THE
HARPER COUNTY
STORY

Gwendoline and Paul Sanders

1968

First Edition, 1968

Printed in U.S.A. by The Mennonite Press
North Newton, Kansas

Dedication

This book is dedicated to all who have ever loved Harper County. It is with fond regret that we finish this book. We will not again find a more warm or generous people.

We like to say, "Harper County is where the West begins!"

Gwendoline and Paul Sanders.

THE HARPER COUNTY STORY

I know there is a prairie green
        Beyond the farthest hill,
I know there is a river
        Where I may drink my fill,
I know there the sun shines
        And the winds are never still,
So I must follow, follow,
        Beyond the farthest hill.

CONTENTS

GEOLOGICALLY SPEAKING

The oldest rocks exposed in Harper County are Permian rocks, about 200 million years old. These are the red rocks which are exposed throughout the county. They are composed principally of siltstone and sandstone which were deposited in a shallow brackish sea. The red color is believed to be derived from weathering of the materials prior to their transport and deposition. These Permian deposits have been divided into three formations: the Ninnescah Shale occurs in eastern Harper County, the Harper Siltstone which lies next above the Ninnescah is exposed in Central Harper County and the Salt Plain Siltstone which is exposed in western Harper County.

Younger rocks of Permian age which are now exposed in Barber, Clark and Comanche counties to the west were probably deposited but were eroded from Harper County when these rocks were exposed to weathering for a long time.

Lower Cretaceous rocks may have been deposited in Harper County. However, if they were, they have since been removed by erosion. The nearest present exposure is in southeastern Kiowa County. Following this deposition, if it occurred, Harper County has remained a land area to the present time.

Overlying the Permian deposits in Harper County are Pleistocene deposits. These deposits are composed of silt, clay, sand and gravel deposited by streams which flowed through the area. Much of the material comprising these Pleistocene deposits originally came from the Rocky Mountains; however, none of it was derived from the mountains directly, for materials from the mountains was first deposited in older deposits in western Kansas and then picked up by Pleistocene streams and redeposited in Harper County.

The age of Pleistocene deposits in Kansas range in age from about one million years to the present. During the Pleistocene, sometimes called the ice age, four periods of continental glaciation occurred in North America and although in none of these glaciations did the gracier reach Harper County the climatic changes which occurred are reflected in the deposits in the county.

The Volcanic Ash which occurs in small isolated deposits in the county is of Medial Pleistocene age and is somewhat less than 500,000 years old. This ash is believed to have been derived from eruption of volcanoes in Northern New Mexico. The ash was carried into the area by southwesterly winds and concentrated into the presently seen deposits by streams.

The brackish seas in which the Permian "red beds" were deposited were not good habitats for aquatic life and supported only very limited fauna. Fossils, except for those of a minute brine shrimp, are absent in the Kansas "red beds."

Since this area was a land area during the Pleistocene one would expect to find fossils of animals which lived on the land in this area. The Mastodon tooth reportedly found in Harper County bears this out. Certainly animals both large and small roamed the Harper County area but the fossils are not common.

Salt

Salt underlies all of Harper County and the salt beds extend for many miles in all directions from the county. These beds are known as the Wellington salt beds, and extend from Sumner County northward to Ottawa County, westward to Trego County, and southward to Meade County. These beds, except in the eastern part where much of the salt has been removed by solution in ages past, are quite thick.

At Anthony salt occurs first at a depth of 950 feet and is continuous to about 1,350 feet. About 400 ft. of rock salt is present.

Copper

UNITED STATES DEPARTMENT OF INTERIOR GEOLOGICAL SURVEY

"A study was made of the copper content of the Ninnescah Shale and the Milan Dolomite Member of the Wellington Formation in south-central Kansas. Five east-west sampling traverses were made across the outcrop in a four county area. Channel samples numbering 411 were analyzed by X-ray spectroscopy for copper. The copper as a mineral malachite, was found to be the highest (6.65 percent Cu as the metal) in the Runnymede Sandstone Member of the Ninnescah Shale in Harper County, Kansas."

It is noted by Geologist Charles K. Bayne of the United States

Department of Interior Geological Survey and State Geological Survey of Kansas, "Should shortages in copper become acute in the future, some copper could be recovered from this area."

Crisfield Diamonds

Many fascinating stones may be found in Harper County. The southwest quarter of the county has yielded more than any other part, here may be found petrified wood, agate, jasper, quartzite, flint and quartz.

The most interesting and romantic stone is the "Crisfield Diamond." The early pioneers sent these stones to Tiffany's in New York for cutting. These diamond-cut quartz rivaled true diamonds in brilliance.

The quartz when found, appears to be a clear pebble, their smooth surface may be explained in that they were tumbled for millions of years on their journey from the Rockies.

Mr. Bayne, geologist, describes "Crisfield Diamonds" as follows: "The Crisfield Diamonds are composed of quartz. Many kinds of quartz are found in this area, the color ranging from perfectly clear to many shades of red, blue, yellow and even black. The clear variety is silicon dioxide and the colored variety contains other minerals in addition to the silicon dioxide. Diamonds are pure carbon and have a hardness of 10 whereas quartz has a hardness of about 8 and would scratch glass but not diamond. Diamonds will scratch both glass and quartz."

Should you go diamond hunting, remember that the Crisfield area is rattlesnake country—don't go bear hunting with a switch!

THE BEGINNING

By James V. Chism

*Department of Anthropology, University of Manitoba
Winnipeg, Manitoba, Canada*

It would be safe to say that few of us appreciate how long what we now call Harper County, Kansas, has been a home for mankind. We tend to think of a century as a long time. However, when we realize that probably men have lived here for more than one hundred centuries, it places our occupation of the land as recent. How many tens of thousands of adventure stories have taken place here; stories of big game hunting, savage warfare, blood feuds, romances, primitive political maneuvers, life and death struggles with blizzards and droughts are lost to the past? Archeologists try to probe these years, but we can barely dent the surface.

At this time the earliest human occupants of what is now Harper County are still cloaked in mystery. Evidence from other regions would lead us to believe that sometime around 10,000 years ago ancient big-game hunters, using stone-tipped spears, stalked gigantic, now extinct, elephant-like mammoth and mastodon, as well as larger variety of bison than we know today. Bones of these extinct animals are to be found in abundance throughout this area, but evidence of the early hunters escaped our most relentless searching. These hunters may have deserted this region between 5,000 and 7,000 years ago. This means that we have found no sign of the county's first 5,000 years of human history. Even while some feel that man has been here at least 20,000 or 30,000 years.

Some time around 5,000 ago years a new way of life moved into the area. This may mean that a new wave of immigrants arrived on the scene. Evidence of these so-called "archaic" groups is to be found through the county. It is presumed that hunting was still very important for these groups, but they were now hunting smaller bison and other smaller game. Further-

more, there has been evidence in other parts of the country that
these people spent more time gathering wild grains and other
plant foods. Although we find various tools of these people
throughout the county, there has been no formal archeological
study made of them. It is thought that they moved into the
county from the east and remained in the area until closely
related groups brought in the making of pottery, sometime between 1,500 and 2,000 years ago. It is highly questionable
whether the pottery-making Plains Woodland people were in
this area and if they were whether they brought early crude
ideas of agriculture with them. Much hard work and careful
research is needed in Harper County and surrounding areas
before this question can be answered. There is some evidence in
the county to suggest this. Unfortunately, this one site is buried
under ten feet of dirt and would be difficult to investigate.

There is somewhat better chance that later Middle Woodland people introduced pottery to the early inhabitants of Harper
County. Again, because the prehistory of the county is so little
understood, we cannot say whether agriculture was introduced
at this time. Our strongest evidence for agriculture is related
to a late prehistoric migration from what is now Eastern Oklahoma. A powerful and highly organized group which might
have been the ancestors of the Caddo, Pawnee and Wichita
began spreading into the plains. The expansion of this powerful,
agricultural temple and mound-building nation may have begun
as early as 900 A.D., 1,000 years ago. The interesting question
for people who now live in Harper County is, "When did these
energetic farmers arrive in this area?"

Through the kindness of Mr. and Mrs. Dow Manderville
and with the help of both University of Kansas and local people, the writer has excavated at a small, but important living
site of these people. A sample of burned corn, recovered from
the lower levels of this site, can be dated by the radioactive carbon method.

For some reason, perhaps drought, Harper County was abandoned by these people. Roving bands of hunters operated in the
area when it was settled by the latest migration, our own ancestors.

*   *   *   *

Artifacts Uncovered Near Anthony

From *The Wichita Eagle,* June 20, 1967.

"Ancient artifacts such as bone hoes, stone knives, projectile points, pottery shreds and discarded animal bones have been recovered by archaeologists from storage areas and of a 600-year-old Indian village eight miles southeast of here.

"The artifacts have been recovered by Tom Witty, state archeologist, and three staff men, James Marshall, Tom Barr and Francis Calabreese.

"As Indian villages went, the village near here was a large one, according to Witty. He said the Indians apparently were semi-sedentary farmers and hunters and possibly were related to the Washita Focus, and archeological classification for a cultural group known to have lived in present-day Oklahoma. Witty said the village probably dated back to about 1300 to 1400 A.D.

"Pits from which the artifacts were recovered were scraped open by county road crews."

*   *   *   *

The following was contributed by Thomas A. Witty, archaeologist for the State Historical Society.

"In the last year (1967) we have carried out a series of tests and the excavation of storage pits along a county road which crosses a Middle Ceramic site near Anthony. This has very tentatively been identified as belonging to the Washita Focus. The following is a quote from Waldo R. Wedel's book, "Prehistoric Man on the Great Plains."

"In central Oklahoma we may note first the Washita River Focus, best known with sites in Garvin and Grady counties. The village sites of the Washita River people are situated on stream terraces and upland promontories conveniently near potable water. They consist of remains of square houses with four center posts, and extended, covered entryways, a prepared clay and fire basin; the presence of burned clay with grass and impressions suggest the structures were daubed with clay, if not earth covered as in the Central Plains. Cache pits used secondarily for refuse disposal, and flexed and simi-flexed burials, with or without offerings, are also at these sites, but there is no indication that these communities were fortified. Refuse bone includes bison, deer, antelope, turkey, rabbit, and other forms, betokening a heavy reliance on the chase. Turtle, fish, and mussels were apparently used. There is direct evidence of corn and beans; and agriculture was carried on with the use of the bison scapula hoe with a socket for hafting, the bison frontal horn with a horn core handle, and the digging stick equipped with a point fashioned from the cannon bone of the bison. Metates and Manos were used in food preparation. Various cutting and scraping jobs were performed with triangular, oval, lanceolate, and diamond-shaped chipped stone knives and scrapers, polished celts, and shell scrapers. For skin working there were rib and deer metapodial beaming tools, stone drills and bone awls, needles, etc. Arrow shaft wrenches were fashioned from deer leg bones. Ornaments included bone and snail-shell beads. Stone pines and deer antler headdresses indicates ceremonial or ritual practices. Miscellaneous tools include sandstone awl sharpeners, whetstones, arrow-shaft smoothers, hammerstones, and curved bone squash knives. Pottery was fairly plentiful and surprisingly varied usually tempered with shell or with sand, crushed sherds, or bone. Vessels were mostly plain-surfaced jars, with flat bases and occasional handles; and some pieces were cord roughened. Discs, figurines, and elbow pipes were also made of clay. Chipped stone included Kay County flint as well as Alibates domolite from the Texas Panhandle quarries."

Wedel suggests the dates for the Washita River Focus to be from 1300 to 1600 A.D.

"This cluster of Washita Focus sites which occurs east and south of Anthony is very interesting and represents one of the northernmost known Washita Focus sites.

"I have seen other material from the county representing the Woodland occupation on the plains which would date from around the time of Christ to 800 A.D. This is the period of the first potters, users of the bow and arrow and possibly domesticated plants. Within the county however, the sites near Anthony are certainly the most significant."

TRAILS IN HARPER COUNTY

Much of the story of the trails across Harper County is learned by piecing together bits of information that we believe to be authentic. The Kiowa Trail or Road is the oldest. Chapter (14) 'Camp ground,' gives this route in detail. Following these directions one would cross Harper County from northeast to southwest.

G. A. Root traced the Kiowa Trail on a map for the Kansas Historical Society in 1939. Mr. Root shows the trail as being in a direct line from Wichita to Kiowa. Due to terrain and rivers the trail could not possibly have been as regular as the hypotenuse of a triangle as shown on this map. After many months of research we believe the trail follows the direction given by J. R. Meade, Kansas Historical collection, Vol. X, 1907, 1908.

The Kiowa Trail as used by the settlers is a part of the military road used by thousands of soldiers. The military road would have had to drop almost due south of the Crisfield area to use the landmark, the convergence of the Medicine and the Salt Fork rivers. The Kiowa Trail, as used by the settlers would have continued southwest to Kiowa.

Remnants of the trail have been traced by finding parts of ancient wagons and traveling equipment of the times north of Conway Springs, in Sumner County, as the trail would have made its way to cross the Ninnescah toward points north and east.

A cattle trail crossing can be found today north and west of Argonia, in Sumner County. The trail can be further traced north and east toward the Ninnescah.

We believe that Harper County was a corridor for many foot soldiers as well as cavalry on their way to Camp Supply, El Reno, and Fort Sill in Indian Territory.

The Ellsworth or Cox's Trail was primarily a cattle trail. Wayne Gard, in his book, "The Chisholm Trail," gives Round Pond or Pond Creek, Oklahoma, as the starting point of this particular branch of the trail. The Ellsworth progressed north and east to cross Bluff Creek near Caldwell at Cox's Crossing. The trail took a northwesterly course out of Sumner County to cross Harper County. The exact entrance and exit are unknown but the trail's destination was Ellsworth, Kansas.

From "The Ellsworth Reporter," April 20, 1967
By Francis Wilson
"Gradually resistance of settlers (to cattle herds) forced the Texans to use trails farther and farther west. Abilene made it known that Texas cattle and cattlemen would no longer be welcome there. In Ellsworth County the same battle raged. On March 9, 1872 a group of people at the Thompson Creek schoolhouse formed the 'Ellsworth County Farmers Protective Society.'

"This resistance caused, in 1873, the establishment of a new trail, called Cox's or the Ellsworth Trail and reached Ellsworth by way of Kingman and Ellinwood west of the more settled areas. That year Ellsworth boasted the largest stockyard in Kansas."

The Harper Trail

From *The Harper Sentinel,* April 26, 1883.

"To the stock-growers of the southwest country adjacent and tributary to the above cattle shipping point, the following observations and facts relating to the new trail as lately established by a committee appointed by the citizens of Harper for that purpose, is respectfully submitted. To correct any erroneous ideas that may have been formed relative to the subject, herewith is presented in due season a review of the proposed line of the trail with all facts connected herewith. To intelligently present to our range friends all points of interest bearing upon the subject fully explains the motive of this communication. The report will be found to be free from bias or prejudice. The facts as related were gleaned from the follwing well and favorably gnown gentlemen: O.P. T. Ewell, G. D. Thompson and Jos. Munger. The foregoing named parties have been unceasing in their efforts to establish a trail that would meet the approval of the Western Stockmen who have occasion to drive over this route. In their correspondence it is proposed to recognize the cattleman's interest and post them thoroughly regarding the very important matter which interest the readers of the section mentioned. It is useless to argue necessity of an inland shipping point for domestic livestock. To Harper the shipping point of the past and present will be our aim in this letter."

A map from the above news item sketched the trail as follows: one branch came in from the west near Sharon, in Barber County, the next fork came in from the southwest near Crisfield, a south fork came up from the south county line below Corwin. These forks converged near Attica and continued east into Harper and the stockyards.

Opening Trail

Anthony Journal, Sept. 19, 1878.

Preparations are being made by the merchants for opening a trail to the herding range on the Medicine Lodge River in the Indian territory. A subscription list was circulated and a sufficient amount readily obtained for the opening of the road, and at a meeting of the subscribers the contract was let to Charles Metcalf. The party under the guidance of G. W. Vicars, surveyor, started for Drum Camp, at the junction of the Big Sandy and Medicine River. They will cut a furrow on their return, over the route selected and this will soon be a well traveled road, bringing a large amount of trade to the town. The trail will cross the Kiowa road, ten miles to the southwest of Anthony and will also serve to bring travel from that point this way, and it will be a direct route to Wichita.

Sharon, Kansas, June 18, 1968.

Dear Friends,

In regard to the old Long Horn Trail, it came across the top of the cedar hills, then straight east to the north side of Crisfield, then across the county.

Great droves of longhorns used the trail as early as I can remember. Most herds were about 5,000 to 8,000 head. The herd that I remember best came through in 1896 with 16,000 head. They were on their way to Peabody, in Marion County, to be split into smaller bunches and be put on full feed. The herd took all day to pass our house, the cowboys stopped for a drink of water; they all carried six-shooters in their belts. Along with the herd were thirty wagons and a whole herd of saddle ponies.

Outside of a few bands of sheep I believe that the trail was not used after 1897.

Yours resp.
Chauncy McReynolds
Box 24, Sharon, Kansas.

(Author's note): Some called this trail the 'Kiowa Trail.'

Buffalo Wallows

Today in native pastures in Harper County buffalo wallows may still be found. These small saucer-like depressions form pools of water in rainy weather. These indeed were made by buffalos. George Catlin, famed Indian painter and writer, who lived from 1796 to 1872 roamed the wilderness, painted the Red Man and the animals that he saw. Some authorities claim Catlin to be one of the most extraordinary men of the 19th century. He wrote the following about the buffalo wallows.

"The almost countless herds that are sometimes met with on these prairies may yet be seen by any traveler who will take the pains to visit these regions. 'A bull in his wallow' is a frequent saying in this country and has a very significant meaning with those who ever have seen a buffalo bull perform his ablution, or rather endeavoring to cool his heated sides by tumbling about in a mud-puddle. In the heat of summer, these huge animals, which, no doubt, suffer much with the great profusion of their great long shaggy hair or fur, often graze where there is a little stagnant water among the grass, and the ground underneath being saturated with it, is soft, into which the enormous bull, lowered down one knee, will plunge his horns, and at last his head, driving upon the earth, and soon making an excavation in the ground into which water filters from amongst the grass, forming for him, in a few moments, a cool and comfortable bath, into which he plunges like a hog in his mire. In this delectable laver he throws himself flat on his side, forcing himself violently around, with his horns and his huge hump on his shoulders presented to the sides, he plows up the ground with his rotary motion, striking himself deeper and deeper in the ground, continually enlarging the pool, in which he at length becomes nearly immersed, and the water and mud about him mixed into a complete mortar, which changes his color, and drips and streams from every part of him as he rises to his feet, a hideous monster of mud and ugliness too frightful and too

eccentric to be described. It is generally the leader of the herd
that takes it upon himself to make this excavation, and if not
(but another one opens the ground) the leader (who is con-
queror) marched forward, and driving the other from it, plunges
himself into it; and having cooled his sides, and changed his
color to a walking mass of mud and mortar, he stands in the
pool until inclination induces him to step out and give place to
the next in command who stands by ready; and another and
another who advances forward to enjoy the luxury of the wallow, until the whole band, sometimes a hundred or more, will
pass through in turn, each one throwing his body around in a
similar manner, and each one adding a little to the dimension
of the pool, while he carries away in his hair an equal share of
clay, which dries to a grey or whitish color and gradually falls
off. By this operation a circular excavation of fifteen or twenty
feet in diameter and two feet in depth is completed and left for
water to run into."

CAPTAIN NATHAN BOONE

Captain Nathan Boone's trek across Harper County in 1843.

By Nyle H. Miller, Secretary
Kansas State Historical Society.

A party of ninety men under the leadership of Captain Nathan Boone, youngest son of Daniel Boone, the famous Kentucky pioneer, traveled through Harper County in 1843. The company was in the boundaries of present Harper County from May 29 through June 3. These men, in light of present knowledge, were the first white men known to have visited the county.

Harper County, situated as it is, far from the Santa Fe Trail —which was the nation's first transcontinental highway, and ran through Kansas from the northeast to the southwest—cannot possibly share in this history of this famous road. Likewise, it is not likely that Coronado, who visited Kansas land in 1541, ever set foot on Harper soil. Press agents from many Kansas cities and counties maintain that the famous Spaniard tread their respective lands, but no records have been found which establish to any degree of certainty the course he traveled through the state. It is inconceivable to enter Harper County in this controversy, for it has at present less claim to this distinction than some of the others. Neither can the county claim any connection with early explorations of Pike, Fremont and Long whose movements in Kansas are more definitely known, and, who, for the most part, followed the courses of the larger rivers of Kansas, none of which are found in Harper County. Lieutenant Bell went down the Arkansas in 1819 or 1820 going through Sumner and Cowley counties, but it is hardly likely that any of his party reached Harper County.

It remained for Nathan Boone, a captain of the United States dragoons, to "discover" Harper County. He departed from Fort Gibson (Oklahoma) May 14 under orders from General Zachary Taylor to make a "reconnaissance of the Western prairies." His report and diary, now a part of the War Department records, were first published in "Marches of the Dragoons of the Mississippi Valley," by Louis Pelzer, and later, with an accompanying map, in the "Chronicles of Oklahoma," a publication of the Oklahoma Historical Society.

The expedition proceeded in the northwesterly direction from Fort Gibson until it reached the vicinity of the present Medford. Then a northerly course was followed through Harper, Kingman, Reno and Rice counties, returning through the neighboring tier of Barton, Stafford, Pratt and Barber counties, where it again entered Oklahoma.

Captain Boone and party, whose equipment included three wagons, entered Harper County May 29, north of the present Manchester, Oklahoma. If any member of the younger generation doubts the existence of Indians and buffalos in his own backyard, let him read the following accounts from the report and diary of Captain Boone. The report which is a summary of the expedition, tells of meeting a band of Osage Indians and of the encampment with them about two or three miles northwest of the present Bluff City on Pahabee (Bluff Creek). But let Captain Boone tell it:

"We fell in with a party of Osages, thirty or forty in number, accompanied by their families, near the great Salt Plains. We encamped with them and during the night they stole from my camp ten horses, and two mules. Six of these horses, and two mules, were public animals, the remaining four belonging to the officers.

"At this time I had not sufficient proof against them to act promptly with them. The Chief of this party called himself To-wan-da-ha, his interpreter who called himself John, was an Osage, and spoke tolerable English, our camp was on the creek called Pa-ha-bee, a branch of the Red Fork (upper). Having spent several days in trying to recover our stolen horses, visited the Great Salt Plain, but without examining it, and seeing no sign of Ryburn's party I steered north, in order to strike the Santa Fe Trail where it first strikes the Arkansas, intending to revisit the Salt Plains and give it a thorough examination.

"I left To-wan-da-ha and party on third of June, and on the fifth of June, met a small party of Osages among whom were several of To-wan-da-ha's band, one of them riding one of the mules which had been stolen from us on the night of May 29.

This I considered as satisfactory proof of the theft, they knowing their guilt became alarmed and attempted to escape. We seized them, took their arms, and permitted such officers 'at their request' as had lost horses, to replace them with Indian ponies, four of which were taken. I ordered the Osages to show us their camp but could not prevail upon them to do so, and then I told them to go, and bring our stolen horses, and I would restore them their property, but this did not have the desired effect. After encamping on the evening of the 5th, three Osages of the same party visited our camp, and wanted to exchange their horses for the horses which we had taken from them. I again told them to bring my horses, and they should have theirs, with their arms, but without effect."

The horse and mule stealing described by Captain Boone occurred in Harper County and may go down in history as the county's first. The subsequent finding of one of the mules, however, took place after the party left the borders of present Harper County on its way north.

"16th day, 14th day marching. May 29th, Monday. Started at seven, going northwest for some distance over the successive elevations of the prairie, we finally came in sight of an Indian, and two officers started in pursuit and overtook some Osages. They took us to their camp and upon receiving information that one of the Salt Plains was within twenty miles, concluded to encamp on the same stream with them, and get a guide the next day for it. They had killed twenty-five buffalo in and about their camp, so we are now in the buffalo range. The creek on which they encamped flows southeast and is quite a large branch of what we have called Red Fork. They call this creek Pa-ha-bee. We have not seen the buffalo. Our distance was about twelve miles north ten degrees west. (The expedition at the start of this day's march was encamped east of Wakita, Oklahoma. On this day they crossed the present Oklahoma-Kansas boundary line into Harper County and, meeting the Osage Indians, they encamped near them on Bluff Creek, northwest of Bluff City.)

"17th day. May 30th. Tuesday. This morning several horses were missing and evidence of foul play shown by the lariats being cut. In a short time a great disturbance was shown in the Osage camp. They came and reported that the Pawnees had been at camp and had stolen some of their horses as well as

ours. This induced the commander to detach two subalterns and
30 men to follow their trail. This party got off at about half past
6 and followed the Osages on the trail for nearly 30 miles at a
gallop, but there they lost it in a sandy plain filled with buffalo.
After this suspicion was fixed on the Osages, themselves, and the
party returned to camp. The horses taken were picketed in a
second bottom below camp, on the creek—rather out of view of
the sentinel, and so near the Osage camp that no Pawnees would
ever come there for them. This day the party sent in pursuit was
conducted about 25 miles north 80 degrees west and there
crossed a creek, running to the left of some size. (The pursuing
party followed the ridges between Sandy and Bluff Creek. They
passed through the vicinity of present Shook and crossed Sandy
Creek near Crisfield before returning to their camp near Bluff
City.)

"18th day. 15th day's marching. May 31st Wednesday. The
Osages were informed this morning that it was believed that
they were the horse thieves and they must give up the horses or
they could not go on their hunt. They said they would go and
put us on the Pawnee Trail. Camp was accordingly broken up
and all the Indians taken with us; after traveling ten miles west
and encamped on a deep gully running southwest toward the
West Forks—from the ridge near this the Osages showed the
trail of the shod horses and not a single pony track was among
them and the trail diverged to the left entirely off of the route
they led the Dragoons on yesterday; showing conclusively that
they led the party on the right side of the ridge, on a false track,
while on the left these men were running off our horses. A
butcher knife was found in camp where one of the horses was
cut loose, and one of the pursuing party of yesterday handed it
to the chief saying he had found it on the chase, and asked him
if it belonged to the Osages—'Oh, yes wa-sh-ay.' But when told
it had done the mischief he said his trader had traded with the
Pawnees, and they had knives like the Osages and he was mis-
taken. The camp set up at the end of this day's march was located one or two miles southeast of Shook."

Boone and his men followed the horse thieves across southern
Harper County into Oklahoma and the Salt Plains. Finally they
decided to give up the chase and continue the northward
journey.

"21st day. 16th day. day's marching. June 3rd., Saturday.

Started at 7 a.m. and marched twenty miles north and encamped on some ravines of the Shaw-wa-cos-pay river, where
there was spring water—our journey today was through the
prairie, passing but two or three cottonwood trees all day. The
water was sulphurous and the rock gypsum and the red sandstone dipping to the southeast very slightly. The gypsum is
mixed with sandy marl and the strata very friable, with occasional lumps of solid gymsum, each lump containing gypsum
in its three forms. An efflorescence was observed over this marl
of some whitish salt which the horses were fond of; it was not,
however, from common salt. Part of the day, the soil was red,
the latter part of the day we came to a yellowish alluvium on
the red. Our camp was on the red again from the hills back of
the camp the view was extensive, looking over the country for
30 miles in every direction. We passed great quantities of prairie
dog towns—no buffalo—a few deer, hares, and antelope—one
wild turkey was seen near our camp tonight. About four miles
from camp passed the Pa-ha-bee creek, called so by the Osages
from the man who was killed there. A horse of 'H' Company
was missing this morning." (This day's journey carried the party
north from its camp near present Shook to the present Harper-
Kingman boundary line in the vicinity of Duquoin. It is not
possible in this description to give the exact place of encampment but it is likely that it was on the Kingman side of the
boundary. On this journey the soldiers passed very near the
present Crystal Springs. The Account of this journey north
through west central Harper County is especially interesting.
Prairie dogs, deer, hares and antelopes were observed. Also the
scarcity of timber was noted by Captain Boone.)

EARLY HARPER COUNTY HISTORY

Historical Sketch of Harper County by B. F. Lee of Anthony.

From "Historical Atlas of Harper County, Kansas"—1886.

Harper County is centrally located on the line of the State, and is one of the thirty-seven counties blocked out on the maps and bounded by the general statutes of the State in 1868, page 236; by statutory act, January, 1872, the legislature in creating Kingman County detached six townships from the north line of Harper and attached them to Kingman. In 1873 townships 31-35, Range 10 west were detached from Harper and added to Barber leaving Harper in its present form, about 26 3/4 by 30 miles. This includes of the Osage Diminished Reserve a tract 24 by 30 miles, and of the Cherokee Neutral Strip a tract about 2 3/4 by 30 miles. The former was sold to actual settlers, 160 acres each, at $1.25 per acre, under the pre-emption laws in trust for the Osage Indians, except sections 16 and 36 which belonged to the State and were sold for school purposes at not less than $3.00 per acre. Of the latter there were 49,258 acres in this county, but there was very little of it sold until the government offered it at public sale at $1.00 per acre, on August 12, 1878. It continued on the market at private entry at that price until it was all sold, being bought principally in large tracts by speculators.

Harper County is in comparatively a low altitude of about 1,325 feet above sea level in the center of the county. It is bounded on the north by Kingman County, on the east by Sumner County, on the south by the Indian Territory, and on the west by Barber County. It is about the most desirable tract of country for pleasant and profitable homes that can be found on all the great Osage belt, having been owned, but never appreciated by many of the Aborigines, and later by the more civilized nations of France and Spain.

Its Early History

Coronado, Marquette, Joliet, Lewis and Clark, Pike, Long, Fremont, the Santa Fe trader and the California gold hunter all had their days of exploring this vast sterile plain, each realizing that somehow and somewhere in the West there was an indefinite region of the Sandy Desert, but each successively reduced its limits until by government survey and the opening up of the country the Great American Desert scarcely has an existence except in the minds of the ignorant or superstitious or on the pages of some ancient geography. In a treaty with Spain in 1819 the United States treated away all their claim on Texas, including all that portion of Kansas west of the 99th meridian and south of the Arkansas River. When Mexico achieved her independence in 1824 this tract passed into her possession, and Texas in turn, on gaining her independence in 1836, claimed this as a part of her domain, which claim was confirmed in the treaty between the United States and Mexico at the close of the Mexican War in 1848, and was finally ceded to the United States in the treaty with Texas in 1850 at which time the United States paid Texas $10,300,300 for this and other lands.

In the year 1540 General Francisco Coronado, governor of one of the northern provinces of Mexico, with over 10,000 men marched from Mexico in a northeast course across Kansas to a point on the Missouri River in about 40 degrees north latitude, set up the cross and took formal possession in the name of the emperor of Spain, and returned to Mexico. His route lay just north of Harper County, crossing the Arkansas River just above Wichita at the mouth of the Little Arkansas. These are the first white men we have any record of in this country. It was then the home of the most powerful Indian tribes of which we have any account; some of them that then numbered two or three thousand in a village are now extinct or have only a handful to preserve their name. In Lieutenant Pike's Account of his explorations of the great West, he says, in reference to the Great American Desert, "I conclude that this country never was timbered, as the aridity of the soil and so few living streams, the channels being generally dry during the growing season, and the summers do not afford moisture enough to support a growth of timber, and I think these vast plains of the West may become equally celebrated with the Great Sahara Desert of Africa. I saw in various places tracts of many leagues where the wind had thrown up the sand in all the fanciful forms of the ocean's waves, on which not a particle of vegetation ever grew." Thus those brave men who first crossed Kansas little dreamt of the greatness, the grandeur and beauty that was to grow out of the dry, parched, sterile country upon which they then looked.

In the beginning of the present century the Santa Fe trade was in its glory. Many and varied were the fortunes of that trade as well as those of the California gold hunter. Many hazarded their lives and property and lost all, while others became rich in a few short months. Captain Bicknell, a Missouri merchant, who, on his second trip to Santa Fe, in crossing Kansas attempted to make a cut off with twenty or twenty-five men, it is supposed in Meade and Finney counties, traveled two days without water, were reduced to the desperate extreme of killing some of their animals and drinking their blood. Many of them had given up all hope and lay down to die, when a large buffalo ran up toward them wet from the Cimarron River. They killed him and with the water from his stomach, saved the weaker ones until water could be procured from the river to save the whole party. It is estimated that not less than 90,000 people crossed Kansas in less than twelve months in 1849 and 1850. But of this vast army of fortune hunters none dared to stay here or pull aside the curtain and look into the future of this country. It was not for them. But dazed by the enchantment of the fairyland of fortune in the distance, their trains moved on in one unbroken procession "farther West."

In 1808, the Osage Indians ceded their land in Missouri to the United States, and were granted a large but rather indefinitely bounded tract of land in Kansas. After 17 years of peaceful but unprofitable possession, it became necessary to find new homes for many of the tribes in the East. A large part of the Osage grant was fixed upon for that purpose, and in a treaty, June 2, 1825, the Osage tribe ceded all their land to the United States, except that belt in southern Kansas known at this time as the Osage ceded and reserved lands. The lands were fifty miles wide north and south, by 276 miles east and west; the east end being 25 miles west of the east line of Kansas, or about one mile west of the line between ranges 21 and 22 east, and extended west to a line about one mile west of the line between ranges 25 and 26 west of the sixth principal meridian, for which the United States was to pay the Osage Indians $7,000 annually, for the twenty year period.

During General Jackson's administration, the United States, by an act of Congress May 26, 1830, provided for the organizing of the Indian Territory, setting apart for that purpose all that tract of country north and east of Red River, west of Arkansas and Missouri, this tract being 600 miles north and south, by 200 miles east and west, surveyed and laid off by Isaac McCoy, including the present Indian Territory, Kansas and Nebraska. The Osages continued to hold and hunt over this tract, always remaining loyal to the government, rendering all the assistance they could in the first struggles of the government for life and liberty, and in the Rebellion raising one regiment under the Stars and Stripes. Many of them, including White Hair, their venerable chief, were converts to the Christian. After the close of the Rebellion in September, 1865, the Osages treated away and sold to the United States a body of land off the east end of their reservation, 30 miles east and west, by 50 miles north and south, extending west from the southeast corner to a point about one mile east of where the Verdigris River crosses the south line of Kansas. This is called the Osage Ceded Lands for which the government paid them $300,000 to be placed in the Treasury of the United States, to their credit, at five percent interest to be paid semi-annually in cash. No pre-emption or homestead entries were allowed on this land.

By the same treaty, September 19, 1865, the Osage Indians ceded to the United States a tract 20 miles wide off the north side of the remainder of the reservation, its entire length from east to west to be held in trust, surveyed and sold by the government for their benefit at not less than $1.25 per acre. This 20 mile strip is the Osage Trust Land, and with the balance remaining, 30 miles wide, known as the Osage Diminished Reserve, was surveyed and sectionized in 1871, and held in trust by the government and opened for settlement under the pre-emption laws.

Harper County, having been bounded by the legislature of 1868, with many other counties in Kansas, attracted little or no attention until 1873, when a giant scheme of swindling struck the brains of some villains on the border of Missouri and Kansas. These men met at Baxter Springs, Labette County, Kansas, early in 1873, and planned the organizing of new counties in

southern Kansas. Wiggins, a grocer at Baxter Springs, agreed
to furnish what funds he could raise out of his stock while his
partners, Boyd and Horner, were to "chip in" liberally of what
they possessed, which consisted principally of their experience in
villainy and fraud. With the proceeds of Wiggins' property, they
set out for Harper County, meeting on their way George Lotus,
a trapper whom they persuaded to join them as guide. After a
short survey and hunt for the center of the county, they located
on Rush Creek, a small branch of Bluff Creek on what proved
to be in Township 32 south, range 7 west of the sixth
P.M., though it is believed they never knew the description
of the land, as they gave no numbers of land in their records.
They built a frame house 16 by 18 feet, dug a well and opened
out on their infamous work. They set up Buffalo bones for
houses and naming the residents by consulting their very fertile
brains or copying city directories, went through the mockery of
enumeration in due form. They petitioned Gov. Osborn, asking
for the enumeration of Harper County (petition dated July 13th,
1873) and asking for the appointment of John Davis for special
census taker; H. H. Weaver, H. P. Fields and Samuel Smith
for special county commissioners, and Daniel Holson for special
county clerk, stating in said petition that the city of Bluff City
was centrally located in the county, and being the largest and
most important town in the county, with good water and timber,
asked that it be assigned the temporary county seat of Harper
County.

On the 16th day of September, 1884, W. M. Matheny and
Thomas S. Jones were appointed by the presiding officers in the
two houses of the legislature as commissioners to investigate the
frauds and ascertain the facts in relation to the organization and
bonded indebtedness of Comanche, Harper and Barber counties. These commissioners made a majority report, but Attorney
General A. L. Williams made a minority report. In the first
report the committee finds "As to the county of Harper that on
the 13th day of July, 1873, a petition purporting to be signed
by forty citizens, householders and legal electors of Harper
County, sworn to by T. J. Jones, J. D. Mains and J. G. Howe,
three of said county, as provided by law, was made out in due
form and presented to the Governor, setting forth that there
were at that time 600 bona fide inhabitants in Harper County,
and asking that said county be organized under the laws of the

State of Kansas." The Governor accordingly appointed special
county officers, appointing John Davis, so named, to take the
census of the county; and his census, with 641 names with petition relating to the organization of the county, was filed in the
office of the Secretary of State, August 20, 1873. The Governor
then, as required by law, declared Harper County organized.
The committee further states that, "It is our opinion that there
never have been forty bona fide inhabitants in Harper County;
that gross and inexcusable frauds have been practiced by those
who engaged in planning and procuring the organization of
said county, . . . and that the names as reported by said census
taker are forgeries. In their report as to the indebtedness is
$40,000; that $25,000 of the debt is for courthouse bonds, and
the remaining $15,000 is for funding debt; that the courthouse
bonds were filed in the office of the Auditor of State, March 12,
1874, and the funding bonds April 4, 1874; that there is not
nor has there ever been a courthouse in the county, and that
we do not know what has become of the bonds, but have heard
that they were sold in St. Louis market, and that the money
used by the individuals selling them for their own use and not
one dollar used for the purpose proposed for the benefit of
Harper County. There is no record of the time or place of
voting the bonds or proof that an election had been held in the
county. No county books were ever seen or persons claiming
to be officers of said county." Attorney General Williams, in his
minority report, says: "It is not pretended that Harper County
ever had a bona fide inhabitant in it; it is doubtful if even the
bond makers themselves were in the county when the bonds
were made"; and as to the amount of indebtedness, he gives
it as above stated by the committee.

In view of these facts it is not strange that Harper County
should be slow to settle and take a respectable stand among the
southern counties of Kansas, as its merits demanded. It required
a good degree of nerve and far-seeing penetration into the future
to attempt to settle it in the face of all the opposing features
and counter evidences, but these qualities were the predominant
makeup of the settlers of Harper County in 1877. It was left
for such a man as G. M. Goss who had already blazed the way
and helped to overcome mountains of opposition to other settlements in other States, to first look it over with an eye to bona
fide settlement. In the fall of 1876, with canteen, picket rope

and pony, he examined it thoroughly and reported. It was left for a small band of home seekers, consisting of Goss, Glen, Snyder, Barton, and a few others from Bloomfield, Iowa, about fifteen persons, men, women, and children, first to strike soil of Harper County as a nucleus for a bona fide settlement, stopping at the point where Harper City now stands, and laying out a town there on the 6th day of April, 1877. It was left to a small number of brave men and women in 1877 and 1878, who were willing to give up comfortable homes, with all that home means, in the older States, and identify themselves with and experiment beyond the limits of civilization, and brave the dangers that had so far intimidated all who had attempted to settle this county. It was left for them to prove that God had assigned —that this county was not created for a waste spot alone, but that it was capable of being developed into and supporting a higher type of civilization than the vast herds of wild animals and no less wild men that had had dominion over it for ages past.

The tourist, trapper or cattleman that passed this way then looked upon it as good for nothing except the short buffalo grass that fed their herds, and repeatedly said that the storms and drouths would drive every family out of the county in less than one year, and that this county was only intended for buffalo and Indians. Up to this time there was nothing to be seen but one unbroken expanse of prairie, with here and there a group of wild horses or antelope. The American people had not heretofore heeded it, but the buffalo and Indians did; hence it was adapted to their use only. All the rain that fell on these prairies then came in storms and passed quickly off, leaving the short, stiff grass dry and nutritious. But the same Creator that made the sterile plain, the buffalo and Indian, made the higher life with all its happy effects; every atom has its design and must fill its place in the great drama in world's history; and the decree that "The desert shall blossom as the rose" was as divinely spoken and as surely fulfilled in regard to Harper County as that man, civilized, intelligent, should rule over the inferior creation, and develop and use them for his own benefit as far as consistent with the Creator's will.

The trader or tourist that passes on the same old trail now is met on every side by beautiful villages and cities; comfortable, happy homes, groves and orchards, fragrant fields of waving grain as far as the eye can reach. To the frontiersman, the hunter or cowboy, it seems a fiction or mirage. They had always looked upon this country as being created for a waste spot, for the boundary of civilization, the playground of the storm king or the battlefield of wild beasts and wilder men. They told us in 1877 that we were beyond the rain belt; that it was a curse and shame to plow this land, and especially a great hazard of money and life to bring families to starve to death. But times have changed. The desert is transformed into an Eden of roses, fruits, fields, orchards and groves. Schoolhouses, churches, villages and cities are the growth of a day; and along the valley where the trapper or trader last camped, hunted or traded, he now looks with doubtful amazement at the great iron horse speeding on impatiently, transporting his precious cargo of life and fortunes from one city to another on his shining track of steel. Things have changed—the climate, soil, grass, people, all have changed. The once parched sandy plain has become a deep, rich bed of loose vegetable loam, which will now absorb all the water that will fall in a week of steady rain. It was no longer a sterile or a desert land. The little ground squirrel, the gopher and the prairie dog increased and multiplied until they literally filled the surface of the earth, and in preparing their homes they pulverize the surface, burrowing deep and throwing up the sub-soil on the top; every pound of soil thus thrown up covering its portion of grass, causing it to rot, thereby making double the amount of the finest vegetable loam that amateur gardener ever put his trowel into.

These openings act as arteries to convey the surplus water into the body of the starved earth, bring into new life an immensely rich but starved soil, eagerly inviting the skilled husbandman to put in his plow or spade.

The beginning is known and truthfully tested by published statistics, and is far beyond the best judgment of the most sanguine of the first settlers. This is the country where you can plow from one end of the field to the other without striking stick or stone; where there is no time lost in clearing or fencing and but trifling cost for land. This is the land that has been prepared by the Creator for a people that were being prepared for it.

Among the many new counties that were offering special inducements to home seekers in the West, none deserved greater and few have had more universal praise from all who know it. That so fair and fertile a spot should so long remain unknown would at first seem a mystery; but to those more intimately acquainted with its early history it is easily traceable to two or three causes, viz.: First, the first impression that it was a sterile and drouthy plain. Second, there was no railroad or corporation interested in advertising its merits, but rather in depreciating them. Third, its fraudulent organization and pretended bonded indebtedness of 1873. This county is in a lower altitude than any of the counties north and west of it; for this reason and also on account of the abundance of surface water it has had, it will continue to have more rainfall than the more elevated counties.

The general course of the streams is from northwest to southeast. The Chikaskia through the northeast corner, Bluff Creek through the center and Sand Creek through the west, with their numerous tributaries, water the county most perfectly with the best quality of clear soft water. Though almost destitute of native groves, yet whenever and wherever permitted and protected from prairie fires, native timber springs up spontaneously, being principally cottonwood with some willow, hackberry, walnut and ash. This in addition to the universal desire and effort to plant trees is rapidly supplying this deficiency. The surface is beautifully undulating, sometimes approaching abrupt hills or ridges interspersed with the finest stretches of valley and bottom lands to be found anywhere in the West, with one striking peculiarity, that the hills and the bottom lands are almost equally fertile, there being no line of distinction. The soil is a dark brown slightly sandy vegetable loam, of inexhaustible fertility, varying in places to a reddish, and in other places to an almost black shade.

Though the farm lands are entirely free from stone or gravel, yet there is an abundance of good building stone in many places, soft and easily cut or sawed when first taken from the quarry but hardening on exposure to the air until it becomes very durable.

Some of the best banks and hotels in the county are built of this stone.

Railroads

There are two main trunk railroads crossing the county from east to west. The Southern Kansas, passing west from Wellington in Sumner County, enters Harper County eight and a half miles south of the northeast corner of the county, passing Danville, Harper, Crystal Springs, Attica and Crisfield, entering Barber County ten miles north of the southeast corner, passing Hazelton to Kiowa, the present terminus, near the State line.

The St. Louis, Fort Scott and Wichita Railroad leaves Wichita in a southwestern course, crossing the first road at Argonia about two miles from the west line in Sumner, and enters Harper County about one and a half miles south of the Southern Kansas Railroad, passing Freeport and Midlothian to Anthony, the present terminus.

First Settlement

The first settler in the county was M. Devoure and family, on Bluff Creek in the southeast corner of the county, early in 1876. About the same time, John Lamar and Henry E. Jesseph settled on the Chikaskia, near where the railroads now cross the county line on the east. These were the men that G. M. Goss found in the county when he visited it in the fall of 1876, looking for a location for a colony; but before the colony arrived, in the spring following, there were a number of claims marked and some permanent settlements. Among them might be named E. McEnany, Martin Lewis, F. B. and S. S. Singer, in the southeast; and G. W. Francis and Silas Burt, in the northeast corner, on the Chikaskia, in the winter of 1876 and 1877.

Organization

The county was organized in 1878 by the appointment of the following officers in August: E. McEnany, sheriff; H. E. Jesseph, Clerk; R. S. Dawson, Probate Judge; R. W. Kirkpatrick, Attorney; H. C. Fisler, Register of Deeds; L. J. Rinehart, Treasurer; B. F. Lee, Surveyor; R. H. Lockwood, Superintendent of Public Instructions; T. H. Stephens, of Anthony, J. B. Glenn, of Harper, and F. B. Singer, of the southeastern part of the county, as County Commissioners. But Glenn declined to serve; so there were but two commissioners till the regular election in November, 1878.

A majority of the officers favoring Anthony as the most central place offering any accommodations for officers, they convened there August 26th, 1878, as the first legal officers of the county. A writ of quo warranto was at once brought, by common consent of all parties and by request of the Governor, to test the validity of the Governor's appointments; the result of which was, the appointments were sustained by the Supreme Court.

At the meeting of the Commissioners the following was ordered spread upon the records:

"To All Whom It May Concern—Know ye, that we, the County Commissioners of the County of Harper, state of Kansas, did on the first day of our first session as Commissioners of said county, at Anthony assembled, this the 26th day of August, 1878, procured conveyance and made diligent search for the alleged town of Bluff City, supposed to be the county seat of said county. And be it further known that we failed to find any town or village or anything pertaining to a town or a village, nor did we believe that there was any such place in said county.

"Therefore, we do hereby designate the town of Anthony, in the county of Harper aforesaid, as the temporary county seat of said county.

T. H. Stephens, Chairman

F. B. Singer, Commissioner."

At the first meeting of the Commissioners, they divided the county into three Commissioners' districts and laid the county into eight voting precincts, with the following place for voting: Chikaskia, J. W. Cleous's: Harper, at Harper; Lake at Cooper's ranch; Silver Creek, at B. H. Freeman's; Anthony, at Anthony; Ruella, at Dr. Perry's; Stohrville, at S. G. Reid's; Spring, at L. Cooper's.

The first county seat election took place in November, 1879. The county then had between 800 and 900 legal voters, while the returns showed up 2,960 votes—which did look a little suspicious; and some said there were unscrupulous frauds practiced in some precincts. Instead of canvassing the votes, they left the ballots in the poll-boxes until they could get proper legal advice, but afterward, when opening the boxes, found them empty.

The people of Anthony and Harper both made a move at about the same time, applying for an alternative writ of mandamus to compel a canvass of the vote, the Anthony folks claiming there were at least three townships in the south end of the county that had cast strictly a legal vote, which it is believed now were the only townships exempt from fraud. They were Ruella, Stohrville, and Silver Creek. The Harper party moved to all clauses charging fraud. This motion was overruled by Justice Brewer, of the Supreme Court, on the ground that 2,960 votes were too many for 800 electors to cast. But in a short time, R. B. Shepard, deputy county attorney, secured an order for a count from the old tally sheets, and the result was found to be in favor of Anthony.

The following is from "Andrea's History of Kansas, 1886."

"The earliest settlement was by M. Devoure and family, H. E. Jesseph and family, John Lamar and family, William Thomas and family, all of whom were settled near the east line of the county in 1876. No further settlement until the arrival of the party who laid out and built Harper City. The first wedding in the county took place in Harper, on Sept. 22, 1878, and united Dr. J. W. Madara and Miss Mary Glenn. The second wedding was also celebrated in the Glenn House, at Harper, and joined W. S. Forry and Miss Francis Glenn. The first birth was that of a child of Mrs. H. E. Jesseph.

"On July 10, 1880, Harper and Chikaskia townships voted on the question of subscribing to the stock of the S.K. & W. Ry. (now the K.C.L. & S.K.). The vote was strongly in favor of the road, standing 153 to 5 in Harper and 102 to 22 in Chikaskia. The amount voted was $28,000, of which Harper had $16,000 and Chikaskia $12,000. The road was built at once, and is now running to Harper.

"On January 31, 1881, Chikaskia Township decided by a vote of 65 to 15 to dispose of its railway stock at 65 cents on the dollar. Feb. 1, 1881, Harper Township decided upon the same course by a vote of 137 to 8."

No one can now realize the hardships and the deprivations endured by these early pioneers. No Indians were reported in the county since the time of the fraudulent organization until after it had been settled several years, but gaunt hunger stalked abroad and frequently confronted the most industrious and enterprising. At one time, when there were eight families West of the Chikaskia, the supply of provisions gave out. Wellington was the nearest trading point, but the Chikaskia River and Slate Creek were past fording. As the situation grew desperate, Wm. Thomas and another gentleman, obtaining a trusty yoke of oxen, started for Wellington. Arriving at the Chikaskia they unhitched the cattle, tied one end of a lariat rope to the cattle's yoke, and the other end to the wagon tongue, swam and drove the cattle to a sandbar, pulled the wagon over, and in the same way crossed the sandbar to the other side. They also had to swim Slate Creek. A fifty pound sack of flour and the same amount of cornmeal was all that could be obtained in Wellington, but they made the best of it.

We now have our production of wheat, corn and stock, but many an early settler will tell you that had it not been for the Buffalo bones found scattered all over the country, for which Wichita offered a ready market, many a family would have gone hungry or been compelled to have deserted their claim. It is impossible to form any accurate estimate of the amount of money realized by the people of this county from this one source, but it certainly was not less than $15,000 or $20,000 and that too at the rate of from $6 to $10 a load, often hauled over 100 miles to market, for when bones became scarce in this county they went out in Barber County, and into the territory to gather them. "Old Reliable" Samuel Thompson, who settled two miles east of Harper, lived in a dugout in the side of a hill, and finding it difficult in crossing the trackless prairie to find his home raised a flag pole, which answered by day, and when returning at night his wife hung a lantern on it to guide him. But with all the hardships and doubts respecting the future many of the early settlers in Harper pronounced the first winter there the happiest of their lives, far from railroads and with mail but once or twice a month, and nothing to do during the winter, they visited and held little social gatherings from which no one was excluded. The establishing of a saloon however, at once divided the people into two factions, and socially "The golden age" of Harper County ended.

UNITED STATES LANDS AND SURVEYS

Standard Atlas of Harper County, 1919.

Up to the time of the Revolutionary War, or until about the beginning of the present century, land, when parcelled out, and sold or granted, was described by "Metes and Bounds," and that system is still in existence in the following States, or in those portions of them which have been sold or granted when the present plan of surveys was adopted, viz.: New York, Pennsylvania, New Jersey, Delaware, Maryland, Virginia, North and South Carolina, Georgia, Tennessee, Kentucky, Texas, and the six New England States. To describe land by "Metes and Bounds," is to have known a landmark for a place of beginning and then follow a line according to the compass-needle (or magnetic bearing), or the course of a stream, or track of an ancient highway. This plan resulted in endless confusion and litigation, as landmarks decay and change, and it is a well-known fact that the compass-needle varies and does not always point due North.

The present system of Governmental Land Surveys was adopted by Congress on the seventh of May, 1785. It has been in use ever since and is a legal method of describing and dividing lands. It is called the "Rectangular System," that is, all its distances and bearings are measured from two lines which are at right angles to each other, viz.: +. These two lines, from which the measurements are made, are the principal Meridians, which run North and South, and the Base Lines which run East and West. These Principal Meridians are established, with great accuracy. Each Principal Meridian has its Base Line, and these two lines form a basis or foundation for the surveys or measurement for all lands within the territory which they control.

All the Principal Maridians and Base Lines in the United States, and from it the territory governed by each Meridian and Base Line may be readily distinguished. Each Meridian and Base Line is marked with proper number or name.

The heavy lines running North and South represent the Principal Meridian. The heavy lines running East and West are the Base Line. These lines are used as the starting points or basis of all measurements or surveys made in territory controlled by the Principal Meridian. Commencing at the Principal Meridian, at intervals of six miles, lines are run North and South, parallel to the Meridian. This plan is followed both East and West of the Meridian throughout the territory controlled by the Meridian. These lines are termed "Range Lines." They divide the land into strips or divisions six miles wide, extending North and South, parallel with the Meridian. Each division is called a Range. Ranges are numbered from one upward, commencing at the Meridian; and their numbers are indicated by Roman characters. For instance the first division (or first six miles) west of the Meridian is Range I. West; the next is Range II. West; and so on, until the territory governed by another Principal Meridian is reached. In the same manner the Ranges East of the Meridian are numbered, the word East or West being always used to indicate the direction from the Principal Meridian.

Commencing at the Base Lines, at intervals of six miles, Lines are run East and West parallel with Base Line. These are designated as Township Lines. They divide the land into strips or divisions six miles wide, extending East and West, parallel with the Base Line. This plan is followed both North and South of the Base Line until the territory governed by another Principal Meridian and Base Line is reached. The divisions or Townships are numbered from one upward, both North and South of the Base Line, and their numbers are indicated by figures. For instance: The first six mile division North of the Base Line is Township 1 North; the next is Township 2 North; then Township 3 North, and so on. The same plan is followed South of the Base Line; the Townships being designated as Township 1 South, Township 2 South, and so on. The "North" or "South" (the initials N. or S. being generally used) indicates the direction from the Base Line.

These Township and Range Lines, crossing each other, form squares, which are called "Townships" or "Government Townships" which are six miles square, or as nearly that as it is possible to make them. These Townships are a very important feature in locating or describing a piece of land. The location of a Government Township, however, is readily found when the number of the Township and Range is given, by merely counting the number indicated from the Base Line and Principal Meridian.

Townships are the largest subdivision of land run out by the United States surveyors. In the Governmental Surveys Township Lines are the first to be run, and a Township Corner is established every six miles and marked. This is called "Townshiping." After the Township Corners have been carefully located, the Section and Quarter Section Corners are established. Each Township is six miles square and contains 23,040 acres, or 35 square miles, as near as it is possible to make them. This, however, is frequently made impossible by, (1st) the presence of lakes and large streams; (2nd) by State boundaries not falling exactly on Township lines; (3rd) by the convergence of Meridians or curvature of the earth's surface; and (4th) by inaccurate surveys.

Each Township, unless it is one of the exceptional cases referred to, is divided into 36 squares, which are called sections. These sections are intended to be one mile, or 320 rods, square and contain 640 acres of land. Sections are numbered consecutively from one to 36. Beginning with section 1 in the Northeast Corner, they run West to 6, then East to 12, then West to 18, and so on, back and forth, until they end with Section 36 in the Southeast Corner. Sections are subdivided into fractional parts to suit the convenience of the owners of the land. A half section, contains 320 acres; a quarter section contains 160 acres, half of a quarter section contains 80 acres, and a quarter of a quarter contains 40 acres, and so on. Each piece of land is described according to the portion of the section which it embraces.

The Government Surveyors are not required to subdivide sections by running lines within them, but they usually establish Quarter Posts on Section Lines on each line of a section. After establishing Township Corners, section lines are next to be run, and section corners are established. When these are carefully located the Quarter Posts are located at points as nearly equidistant between Section Corners as possible. These corners when established by Government Surveyors can not be changed, even though it is conclusively shown that mistakes have been made which cause some sections or quarter sections to be either larger or smaller than others. The laws, however, of all the States provide certain rules for local surveyors to follow in dividing Sections into smaller parcels of land than has been outlined by the Governmental Surveys.

In arranging a Township into Sections all the surplus or deficiency of land is given to, or taken from, the North and

West tiers of Sections. In other words all the Sections in the Townships are made full 640 acres—except those on the North and West, which are given all the land that is left after forming the other 25 sections.

Mistakes of measurement are constantly and almost unavoidably made in running both Township and Range Lines, and if no new starting point were established the lines would become confused and unreliable, and the size and shapes of Townships materially affected by the time the surveys had extended even a hundred miles from the Base Lines and Principal Meridian. In order to correct the surveys and variations caused by the difference of latitude and straighten the lines, "Corrections Lines" or (Guide Meridians and Standard Parallels) are established at frequent intervals, usually as follows; North of the Base Line a Correction Line is run East and West Parallel with the Base Line, usually every twenty-four miles. South of the Base Line a Correction Line is usually established every thirty miles. Both East and West of the Principal Meridian "Correction Lines" are usually established every 48 miles.

THE ESTABLISHMENT OF COUNTIES IN KANSAS, 1885-1903

Reprinted from volume 8 of the Kansas Historical Collections.

The first territorial legislature, held in 1855, passed three acts relative to the establishment of counties in the Territory of Kansas.

The first of these defined the boundaries of thirty-three counties. As the survey had at that time only begun, the definition was made by distances only, the starting point being the main channel of the Kansas River at the point where it crosses the Missouri line. (These counties were in the eastern third of Kansas.)

The second act of 1855 created two new counties: Marion out of a tract of land one hundred miles long and eighteen miles wide, west of Hunter, Butler and the south half of Wise; and Washington, including all the part of territory west of Marion and east of a line drawn north from the northeast corner of New Mexico.

Author's note: "This is the first time in recorded history that definite signs of civilization were seen to be creeping nearer the present site of Harper County. The area of the future Harper

County was included in what was called (1885) Washington County."

By 1857 surveys had progressed so far that it was possible to bound the eastern counties by townships and sectional lines. An act was passed February 20 correcting the boundaries of all counties established in 1885, except Marion, Washington and Arapahoe.

In 1860 new counties were created; Irving out of the north part of Hunter, less a strip of three miles on the east, plus two ranges of townships on the west; Republic and Shirley (later Cloud), Ottawa and Saline, with boundaries as they exist today; Marion, south of Dickenson; Otoe, south of Marion and west of Butler, and Penketon, including all the unorganized territory south of township 16 and between the sixth principal meridian and New Mexico. (General Laws of 1860, pp. 83-87)

Author's note: "The county called 'Washington' in 1855 seems to have been changed to 'Penketon' in 1860. The future Harper County was in the county called Penketon in 1860. Washington County took a permanent place in the north tier of counties between Marshall and Republic."

According to the 'Laws of 1865, p. 44' Marion County was enlarged to include Penketon.

Author's note: "At this time the future Harper County became a part of Marion County."

In 1867 another act provided for the divisions into counties all the unorganized part of the state east of range line 26 west; the counties to be organized when they should have requisite population. The counties created by this act were: Montgomery, Howard, Cowley, McPherson, Sedgwick, Sumner, Jewell, Mitchell, Lincoln, Elsworth, Rice, Reno, Harper, Smith, Osborne, Russell, Barton, Stafford, Pratt, Barbour, Phillips, Rooks, Ellis, Rush, Pawnee, Kiowa, Comanche, Norton, Graham, Trego, Ness, Hodgeman, Ford and Clark. By the same act Seward disappeared and the boundaries of Greenwood, Butler and Marion were changed. Butler took its final form. The south line of Greenwood was pushed nine miles south, to the north line of township 30. Marion was confined to one tier of townships on the south, taken from Butler.

By statutory act, January 1872 the legislature in creating Kingman County detached six townships from the north line of Harper County.

In 1873 Barber County was enlarged by townships 30, ranges 11, 12, 13, 14, and 15 west, which were detached from Pratt and by townships 31-35, range 10 west, which were detached from Harper.

When Harper County was fraudulently organized in 1873 it had its present size of 30 miles by 26¾ miles.

ORGANIZED TOWNSHIPS AND GROWTH OF COUNTY

The board of County Commissioners met at Anthony Aug. 26, 1878, holding commissions under the appointment of the Governor of the state of Kansas dated August 5, 1878. Present were T. H. Stephens and F. B. Singer, the following business was transacted to wit; T. H. Stephens was elected chairman of the board of commissioners. The offices of County Clerk, Treasurer and Register of Deeds were found to be vacant. The following persons were appointed to fill such vacancies. Henry E. Jesseph, County Clerk, L. J. Rinehart, Treasurer, and G. W. Francis, Register of Deeds. The meeting adjourned to meet August 27, 1878.

T. H. Stephens
F. B. Singer

Anthony, Harper County, State of Kansas

To all whom it may concern, know ye all that we the undersigned commissioners of the county of Harper, state of Kansas, did on the day of our first session as commissioners of said county and state at Anthony, assemble this 26th day of August A.D. 1878 procured conveyance and made diligent search for the alleged town of Bluff City and supposed to be the county seat of said county of Harper, State of Kansas, and be it further known that we failed to find any town or village or anything resembling or pertaining to a town or village nor do we believe that there is any such place in said county. Therefore we do hereby designate the town of Anthony, county of Harper, aforesaid as a temporary County seat of said county.

T. H. Stephens
B. F. Singer

Forming of the Justice Precincts

The Chikaskia precinct shall begin at the northeast corner of the county running south to the east corner of sec. 13 (32s-

5w) thence west to the southeast corner of sec. 16 (32s-6w) north to the county line and east to the place of beginning. The voting place shall be the house of J. W. Cleous.

The Harper precinct is as follows- beginning at the southwest corner of the Chikaskia precinct thence running west on the section line to the southeast corner of sec. 13 (32s-8w). Thence running north to the county line thence east to the northeast corner of Chikaskia township; thence south to place of beginning. The voting place shall be Harper City.

The Lake precinct shall be described to wit: beginning at the northeast corner of Harper precinct thence running south to the southwest corner of the Harper precinct, thence west along said line to the west line of the county, thence north to the northwest corner of the county, thence east along the north line of the county to the place of beginning. The voting place shall be Cooper's Ranch.

The Silvercreek precinct shall be described to wit: beginning at the southeast corner of Chikaskia precinct, thence running south to the southeast corner of sec. 25 (33s-5w), thence running west along the section line to the southeast corner of sec. 28 (33s-6w), thence north to the southeast corner of sec. 16 (32s-6w), thence east to the place of beginning. The voting place shall be at Freeman's house.

The Anthony precinct shall be described to wit: beginning at the southeast corner of sec. 16 (32s-6w), thence running south to the southeast corner of sec. 9 (34s-6w), thence west to the southeast corner of sec. 12 (34s-8w), thence north to the southeast corner of sec. 13 (32s-8w), thence east to the place of beginning. The voting place shall be in the town of Anthony.

The Ruella precinct shall be described to wit: beginning at the northwest corner of the Anthony precinct thence south to the southeast corner of sec. 12 (34s-8w), thence west to the western boundary of the county, thence north along the said line to the southwest corner of Lake precinct, thence west along said line to the place of beginning. The voting place shall be at Perry's farm.

The Stohrville precinct shall be described to wit: beginning at the southwest corner of Silvercreek precinct, thence running south to the southeast corner of the county, thence west along the south line of the county to the southeast corner of sec. 16 (33s-6w), thence north to the southwest corner of Silvercreek precinct, thence east to the place of beginning. The voting place shall be S. G. Reid's.

The Spring precinct shall be described to wit: beginning at the southeast corner of Anthony precinct, running south to the county line, thence west along said line to the west line of the county, thence north along said west line of county to the southwest corner of Ruella precinct, thence east on said line to place of beginning. The voting place shall be at Leonard Cooper's.

Author's note— In the ensuing years, as population increased, the eight original townships or voting precincts were gradually broken down into the present twenty of today. The following account is taken from the minutes of the Harper County Commissioners' meeting as new townships were created.

January 3, 1881

A petition was presented by T. A. Smith and 65 others with a census attached certified to by T. A. Smith and F. F. Burnett showing a population of 290 persons. Said petition requests that a new township be formed. Its legal description is as follows: township 32 south, of range 5 west and that its name be called Odell. The petition was granted and it was ordered that the first election for township officers be held at the residence of C. D. Bickford, on the first Tuesday, in February A.D. 1881.

January 5, 1885

A petition signed by W. R. Rowell and others for a new township to be called Blaine. The petition was allowed as follows—a township to comprise all of township 34 south-range 9 west and all of township 35-range 9 west.

July 6, 1886

That the privileges of conveniences and the protection afforded by township organizations may be better enjoyed, the undersigned respectfully petition the honorable body to set off and organize as a new township to be named and known as Eagle township— the following described territory within said Harper County to wit: beginning at the northwest corner of sec. 6 (34s-8w), thence south to the southeast corner of sec. 13 (35s-8w), thence west along the south line of Harper County to the west corner of sec. 18 (35s-8w), thence north along the east line of Blaine township to the place of beginning. This area contains more than 30 square miles and had more than 200 inhabitants and that an incorporated city or town is not included within said limits. Signed by J. Benham and 51 others.

July 6, 1886

To the Honorable, the board of County Commissioners of the county of Harper. Your petitioners most respectfully represent to your Honorable body that they are residents of township 32 south of range 7 west, of the sixth p.m. in the county of Harper, state of Kansas. Your petitioners pray your Honorable body to organize said township 32 above described into a municipal township of the said county of Harper to be known as the township of "Banner." Always excepting and leaving out of said township to be so organized, the city of Harper. For which your petitioners incessantly pray. A.M. Cline and 56 others.

July 1886

To the Honorable board of county Commissioners. Our petition would represent to your Honorable body that owing to the largeness the township of Harper, to the inconvenience of a large number of electors residing in the north part of said township, to attend elections held in said township, and it be to the interest of all the electors who reside in township 31, range 7 west and the west one half of township 31, range 6 west, the present territory being composed of more than 50 square miles and there being in said territory more than 200 inhabitants.

Wherefore it is ordered (G. W. Thompson dissenting) that said Antelope township be set off to comprise all of township 31 range 7 west of the sixth p.m.

January 3, 1887

To the Honorable board of Commissioners, we the undersigned petitioners being residents and legal electors respectfully ask that a new township be formed for municipal purposes consisting of the following described territory to wit: the whole of township 33, range 9 west of 6 p.m. and that the name of said township be "Green township" for which we will ever pray.

April 13, 1887

To the Honorable board of Commissioners of Harper County,

Kansas. We the undersigned would respectfully represent that we are electors residing in township 31 south, range 7 west of the 6 p.m. Harper County, Kansas.

Said township range 7 west of the 6 p.m. contains over 30 square miles and that there are now residing within the limits over 200 inhabitants.

We therefore ask that said township 31 south, range 7 west, 6 p.m. Harper County, Kansas, be made a municipal township and that said township be called "Grant." Signed by B. J. Orange, J. J. Galloway, N. M. Shepherd and G. T. Titus and they were appointed township officers of said Grant township.

April 13, 1887

To the Honorable board of County Commissioners of Harper County, Kansas. We the undersigned would respectfully represent that we are electors residing in township 32 south, range 6 west, 6 p.m. (except that portion included within the corporate limits of the city of Harper, Kansas). That said township 32 south, range 6 west (except that portion within the limits of Harper city) contains over 30 square miles and that there are now residing within the limits of said township as above mentioned over 200 inhabitants. We therefore ask that said township 32 south, range 6 west of the 6 p.m. (except that portion included within the corporate limits of Harper city) be made a municipal township and that said township be called "Pilot Knob" signed H. T. Purcell and 63 others.

July 6, 1887

The township board formed a new municipal township to be known as "Garden," comprising all of township 31, range 8 west, 6 p.m. J. C. Curran was appointed Trustee and C. D. Cutter was appointed Treasurer.

July 6, 1887

The board formed a new municipal township to be known as "Empire," comprising all of township 33, range 8 west, 6 p.m. The officers appointed were Wm. McFarland, Trustee; I. M. Couch, Clerk; and Henry Seibert, Treasurer.

Author's note—The illusive record of the (voting precinct) township "Lawn" caused us to come to the conclusion that it had been formed on July 6, 1887.

On December 7, 1886 the minutes of the Harper County
Commissioners reads to the effect that Harper County was re-
districted as follows: District no. 1—Lake, Harper and Chi-
kaskia. Dist no. 2—Anthony township and city, and east
Ruella. District no. 3—Odell, Silver Creek, Stohrville, Spring,
Eagle, Blaine and west Ruella precinct. Note that the township
"Lawn" is not mentioned. It would appear that it had not been
formed at this date.

Following the July 6, 1887 meeting when "Garden" and
"Empire" townships were formed, a re-districting of the county
followed: District no. 1—Harper, Harper City, Grant, Chikaskia, Lake, "Lawn" and Garden townships. District no. 2—
Anthony, Anthony city, Banner, Ruella, and Empire. District
no. 3—Odell, Silvercreek, Stohrville, Spring, Eagle, Blaine, and
Greene.

"Lawn is included in the record so we are assuming that it
was formed July 6, 1887 at the same time as "Garden" and
"Empire" and through human error it was omitted from the record.

"Lawn was formed out of part of the original townships of
"Lake" and "Ruella." Its legal description reads: All of township 32 south, range 9 west, 6 p.m.

January 30, 1888

To the Honorable Board of County Commissioners of Harper
County, Kansas, we the undersigned being residents and legal
electors respectfully ask that a new township be formed for
municipal purposes consisting of the following territory to wit:
all of township 33, range 6 west, 6 p.m. excepting sections 19-
30-31 and the name of said township is to be "Berlin." Signed
by J. G. Carson and 57 others. The proposed township has a
population of 268 persons.

July 11, 1900

Whereas a petition signed asking that Township 31 south,
range 9 west, 6 p.m. be organized as a municipal township to be
known as "Liberty" township and whereas the board finds that
the petitioners have complied with the law in relation to the creation of townships. Petition was granted. J. Colruian, I. P. Spill-
man and N. Jacobs were appointed trustee, treasurer and clerk
respectively.

Office of County Clerk
Harper County, Anthony, Kansas

Enumeration of Inhabitants on the 1st day of March, 1886

Anthony CITY	3031		As of March, 1888	
Attica CITY	1405		Anthony Township	776
Harper CITY	3472		Anthony CITY	1920
Anthony Township	1731		Attica CITY	616
Blaine	376		Bluff CITY	323
Chikaskia	864			
Harper Township	1364		Banner Township	504
Lake	1169		Berlin	279
Odell	614		Blaine	385
Ruella	1795		Chikaskia	686
Silver Creek	764		Eagle	283
Spring	614		Empire	198
Stohrville	950		Garden	265
			Grant	447
	18,149		Greene	298
			Harper TOWNSHIP	265
			Harper CITY	2114
			Lake TOWNSHIP	507
			Lawn	337
			Odell	582
			Pilot Knob	550
			Ruella	221
			Silver Creek	350
			Stohrville	907
			Spring	429
			Freeport CITY	149
				13,391

HARPER COUNTY, 1948

The approximate population of Harper County is 10,563. Townships listed are Anthony, 491; Banner, 335, Berlin, 172; Blaine, 344; Chikaskia, 183; Eagle, 199; Empire, 184; Garden, 195; Grant, 284; Greene, 209 Harper, 227; Lake, 159; Lawn, 232; Liberty, 173; Odell, 256; Pilot Knob, 275; Ruella, 132;

Silver Creek, 223; Spring, 307; Stohrville, 406; making a total of 4,986.

Cities listed are Anthony, 2,794; Attica, 654; Bluff City, 181; Danville, 109; Freeport, 52; Harper, 1,608; Waldron, 79, with the total of 5,477.

To keep the readers posted on "who's who" in the courthouse now the following list is given: Attorney, Harry B. Davis; Clerk, Marie Connell; Clerk of District Court, Jay B. Pearl; Engineer, Howard B. Stout; Farm Bureau, Elgin R. Button; Probate Judge, R. H. Beebe; Register of Deeds, Ina Brownfield; Sheriff, Hugh Willett; Social Welfare Dept., Georgia Williams; Treasurer, Helen Waldeschmidt; County Superintendent of Schools, John T. Smith. The commissioners are Ray Antrim, W. D. Bellamy and Mel Henderson.

Harper County Officials, 1968

Elected

County Clerk .... Marie Connell
County Treasurer .... Marguerite Ellis
County Attorney .... Wood W. Runyan
County Sheriff .... Floyd L. Snyder
Register of Deeds .... Ethel Morton

Clerk of the District Court .... Florence Stone
Probate Judge .... J. Howard Wilcox
County Supt. of Public Inst. .... John T. Smith

Commissioners

H. C. Grant, Attica, Kansas, 1st Dist.
C. A. Watkins, Harper, Kansas, 2nd Dist.
A. A. Fisher, Anthony, Kansas, 3rd Dist.

Appointed

Jack Scott .... County Engineer
Georgia Williams .... Director of Social Welfare
P. J. Antrim, M.D. .... Public Health Officer
Wesley Poston .... Noxious Weed Supervisor
Grace Gates .... Public Health Nurse
Roger Hendershot .... County Agent

The *Anthony Republican* and The *Anthony Bulletin*,
May 20, 1948.

POST OFFICES

Name	Established	Discontinued	Name changed Location changed*	First Post Master
Albion	Jan. 12, 1883	Dec. 15, 1902	Gourock*	Thos. Elder
Anthony*	June 14, 1878			Geo. W. Maffet
Attica*	July 1, 1880			Virgil J. Beeson
Bluff	Feb. 1, 1887	Jan. 28, 1890	Bluff Creek	Robt. H. Echols
Bluff City*	Jan. 28, 1890			Abram Martin
Bluff Creek	July 24, 1878	Feb. 1, 1887	to Bluff	Samuel G. Reid
Camchester	Feb. 2, 1900	March 31, 1903	from Cameron	Thos. B. Smith
Cameron	June 2, 1893	Feb. 2, 1900	to Camchester	Milton S. Foster
Coleville	Jan. 24, 1881	Jan. 25, 1882	from Odel	Mrs. J. E. Wilson
Cora City	May 22, 1877	June 18, 1877	to Harper	Mrs. Josie B. Glenn
Corwin	Aug. 20, 1883	June 28, 1957		Oscar A. Corwin
Crisfield	Feb. 27, 1885	June 30, 1951	from Otego*	Wm. H. Ranke
Crystal Springs*	Jan. 16, 1885			Mrs. Naomi L. Bukins
Curran	Apr. 27, 1892	Nov. 30, 1903		Mrs. M. E. Curran
Danville*	May 25, 1882		from Coleville	Mrs. E. J. Wilson
Duquoin*	May 23, 1893			Walter E. Fitch
Embry	Dec. 15, 1885	Nov. 5, 1889		William F. Stocker
Ferguson	July 12, 1904	Jan. 30, 1915	(rescinded)	Wm. A. Kuykendall
	Sept. 2, 1915	March 15, 1918		
Freeport*	Sept. 16, 1885		from Mid-Lothian*	L. R. Hill

Post Office	Established	Discontinued	Notes	Postmaster
Goss	May 24, 1892	Sept. 30, 1896		Mary Goss
Gourock	July 30, 1878	Jan. 12, 1883	to Albion* (Estb. in Sumner Co.)	Albert Seavey
Harper*	June 18, 1877	Feb. 18, 1893	from Cora City	Mrs. Josie B. Glenn
Inyo	Nov. 7, 1879	Oct. 14, 1884		Fred O. Hagaman
Joppa	June 30, 1879	Sept. 16, 1885		John A. Squires
Mid Lothian	Apr. 19, 1878	Jan. 24, 1881	to Freeport*	Benjamin Freeman
Odell	Aug. 19, 1878	Feb. 27, 1885	to Coleville	Mrs. S. J. Cleous
Otego	Nov. 23, 1882	June 30, 1904	to Crisfield*	Geo. W. Clark
Ruby	May 13, 1902	May 31, 1889		Leonard K. Belding
Ruella	July 17, 1884	Dec. 31, 1944		Branson Jackson
Runnymede	June 20, 1879	Nov. 18, 1900		Geo. W. Francis
Shook	July 27, 1900	July 15, 1925	(rescinded)	Jesse Montgomery
	June 1, 1901			
Sonora	March 8, 1880	May 25, 1888		Azariah Culbertson
Sullivan	Dec. 15, 1885	June 19, 1886		Shelton Morris
Swan	Dec. 5, 1879	Feb. 27, 1880		Daniel V. Hamilton
Waldron*	Jan. 23, 1902			Howard B. Waldron
Yankton	Aug. 6, 1883	Oct. 14, 1884		Stephen C. Oliver

* Indicate post office still open

Rural Delivery Began in 1904

From *The Anthony Republican,* June 10, 1904.

The free delivery of mail to farmers will begin Friday July 1. Route no. 1 embraces a territory to the northwest of Anthony as far as the farms of B. F. Walter and Henry Shannon. It covers an area of 42 square miles, serves 110 houses and a population of 404 people, and the carrier will travel a distance of 28.5 miles.

Route no. 2 goes in an easterly direction, including the Gwinn farm northeast and the Peter Riley farm southeast. The total miles covered are 29; an area of 36 square miles, serves 105 houses with a population of 420 people.

Route no. 3 goes almost straight south of Anthony to a line two miles from Oklahoma and branches out very little. It covers an area of 44 square miles, delivers mail to 101 houses with a population of 404. The carriers who will carry mail on these routes have not yet been appointed.

July 1, 1904

The carriers for the three rural routes of Anthony have been named as follows: Henry A. Repologle, carrier; Mary T. Repologle, substitute; John L. Hilts, carrier; Mary L. Hilts, substitute; Harry C. Rice, carrier; Rubin S. Miller, substitute.

Mr. Repologle and Mr. Rice are building new rigs for use the first day. Mr. Hilts expects to get a regular wagon, and may have to handle the mail over his route in a buggy until his rig gets here. The new salary of $60.00 per month is effective today.

The *Anthony Republican,* May 1938, reprint from Apr. 18, 1885

Early Mail Service

Anthony's first post office was located in Connell and Wright's grocery store, but in February, 1879, was moved to the hardware store operated by F. N. Hester.

In October, 1878, the mail service from Wellington to Anthony (by way of Oxford) was increased from one to three trips per week.

Bluff Creek (now Bluff City) residents were complaining

in March of 1879, that it took them two weeks to get the Anthony newspaper, and J. S. Soule, editor of the *Journal* (March 27, 1879) explained that "the fault appears to be in the post office at Wellington, through which our mails have to pass and in which they are apparently being unnecessarily delayed."

Jan. 23, 1879

Bluff Creek post office is five miles and a quarter from the south line of the state and one mile and a quarter from the Sumner and Harper county line, and it is the residence of Mr. S. G. Reid, the postmaster. It was established about the first of August, in an answer to the prayers of thirty-eight petitioners. At present it is a special office supplied with mail from Caldwell. But we hope to have a mail route from Caldwell via Doster, Sumner County, and this place to Anthony.

TOWNS

Albion

From Andrea's History, 1883

Albion is a small town on the K.C.L. and S.K. Railway just west of the east line of the county. It was laid out March 4, 1881, on land formerly owned by J. W. Shields, but purchased by a town company of which T. Shields was, and still is, President. The townsite is in the form of a rectangle 1,642 x 720 feet. The first building on the town land was put up by F. E. Beach, the second by Elder Bros. and a third by Portman and Maddy. The post office at this point was formerly known as Gourock, and was kept by Mrs. Seavey. Upon the laying-out of the town, the post office was moved to it but the name was not changed to Albion until the fall of 1882. Soon after the arrival of the Elder Bros., Robert Elder was named postmaster. The town has no churches or secret societies. Its population is about 100.

From *Argonia Argosy,* Dec. 12, 1963

Albion listed the following businesses in 1881: A depot, stockyards, post office (located in the southeast corner of Elder's store), two good stores, livery barn, lumberyard, flour mill, saloon, two blacksmith shops and a drug store, operated by Billy Dewall. School was held in the depot until a schoolhouse could be built. Tom Kaley ran what is agreed by each contributor of Albion history to be a typical, early day "Lum 'n Abner" type store—cracker barrel, gingersnap barrel, and pickle barrel.

Homesites of Alfonso Minnick, Bob Elder, formerly of Michigan, and Mrs. Coryell were noted and Tom Raine was said to have lived in Albion. Jacob W. Fisher's home was built on a knoll just north of the railroad track, and some of the Jesseph family proved up land immediately to the south.

A graduation exercise was held at which Mr. Elder presented a diploma to one graduate, a Bremmer girl. Mr. Schull, an accomplished musician, held music classes in the Albion school.

Mr. John Schon who remembers securing mail at the store post office, says that he tore down the house formerly occupied by Mrs. Coryell just two years ago, and that, while one may still find rock deposits which were no doubt foundations to homes, and he used Mr. Elder's well until two years ago.

Anthony

From Andrea's History, 1883

Anthony, the county seat of Harper County, takes its name from Governor Anthony, who was in office when the town was named. It lies on the edge of a beautiful valley a little over two miles from the geographical center of the country, ten miles from the east end of the county and nine miles south of Harper, the nearest point on the railway.

On April 2, 1871, the town company, which had been formed at Wichita for the purpose of laying out a town at some point near the center of this beautiful county, arrived at Harper City and engaged the services of B. F. Lee, afterward County Surveyor, but then a resident of Harper and a member of the town company. Under his guidance they reached the site of the lone house that served for "Bluff City, the largest place in the county." Following Spring Creek, they reached a point several miles northwest of the present town and began to mark out the streets by running lines with a plow. Lee and Dr. H. Owens were not satisfied with this location and went on horseback to a point near where Anthony now stands. Returning they induced the party to move to a camp one mile south of Anthony. Here they found a beautiful townsite, but also discovering that they were on a school section (section 36) they moved one mile north, where, on April 6, 1878, they located the present town.

The townsite was made to cover 320 acres, and the town company, officered by O. Jennings, President, St. Clair Grey, Secretary, and B. H. Stedman, Treasurer, proceeded to enter the land for pre-emption as a townsite. On June 10, 1878, they proved up through Judge E. Evans, of Sumner County. The first work of the town company was to build a barracks 18 x 30 for the accommodations of emigrants, and to dig three public wells. About a dozen box houses sprang up at once and B. F. Lee moved his house from Harper which was already framed.

The first house of any size was erected by Cornell and Wright, and filled with general merchandise. F. M. Hester opened the first hardware store, C. A. Miller the first drug store. H. H. Kirkpatrick was the first physician, and his brother, W. R. Kirkpatrick the first attorney in the town. The new town grew rapidly and now has a population of 500.

Early in 1879, a petition for the incorporation of Anthony as a city of the third class was drawn up and presented to the Governor. The petition defined the location of the town and states that it has a bona fide population of 275. The petition was granted and an election set for July 18, 1879, resulted in the choice of Henry Holmes, Mayor; Jackson Brock, Police Judge; Jacob Hummel, G. W. Vickers, George P. Morran, Simpson Van Winkle, and David Hinsey, Councilmen. F. M. Hester was appointed City Clerk. Brock failed to qualify, and on November 10, 1879, R. H. Lockwood was appointed Police Judge. On April 5, 1880, occurred the first regular election, but the vote was said to be fraudulent, and the Council, at their meeting April 7, refused to canvass it. There were two sets of officers and two Councils, each claiming to be legally elected. On April 29, acting Mayor Vickers and the Council met in response to a mandamus from the Supreme Court and proceeded to count the ballots cast on the 5th. Their return showed that Jackson Brock had been elected Mayor and W. S. Cade, Police Judge. The officers then took their seats and George Vickers was appointed City Clerk. A straight fight was in order from this time forward and July 5, Vickers was removed and A. S. Lindsay appointed City Clerk. The "outs" however, got the best of the contest and July 22, we find an entry to the effect that H. M. Kirkpatrick was elected Mayor, on April 5, and L. S. Webb, Police Judge. These officers secured their seats and appointed G. W. Bennett, City Clerk.

Anthony Post Office was started in the summer of 1878 (June 14), and G. W. Maffet was appointed Postmaster. The office was supplied by a stage which ran from Wichita to Anthony once a week. Later this service became daily, and when the railway reached Harper a short line was put on from that point and the Wichita line discontinued. Another line runs daily between Anthony and Caldwell. J. M. Lapham followed Maffet and was in turn succeeded by A. S. Lindsay, the present Postmaster. The office was made a money order one in 1880, and the first order purchased August 2 of that year by A. R. Blackburn.

LOCAL MATTERS

District no. 1, which includes the city of Anthony, was formed in 1879, and the public school system inaugurated on May 5, by the engagement of Misses Clara Sherwood and Sarah Bidwell as teachers. The school building was completed in July 1879, at a cost of $1,300. In the summer of 1882, two large wings were added at a cost of $1,000. Funds for both these outlays were secured by the issuance of district bonds, which were sold to the Secretary of State at par.

The first regular Church society was the Congregational, which was organized in 1879, with a membership of nineteen. Its first pastor was Rev. Mr. Hobbs, who was succeeded by Rev. T. D. Childs, the present pastor, in October, 1880. The first services were held in the old courthouse, whence they were removed to the schoolhouse, and later to the church building. This building was put up in 1880 at a cost of $1,700, and has a seating capacity of 250. The Union Sabbath School, started in 1878, has always been connected with this church, and in 1882, had an average attendance of 120. A partition was effected Jan. 1, 1883, and the school now numbers about 70. It is in charge of O. Jennings.

The METHODIST EPISCOPAL church was formed in the fall of 1878, by Rev. W. H. Mock, who gathered nine members. Occasional services were held by W. H. Mock and J. D. Hamilton, the earliest being held at the residence of B. F. Lee. Later the old courthouse and the school building were used. In the fall of 1882, work was begun on a church edifice, which was completed in 1883, and dedicated in January 28, at a cost of $2,500. J. W. Anderson was the church's first regular pastor. A Sabbath School was organized January 1, 1883.

THE CHRISTIAN CHURCH was organized in 1880, with eighteen members. It has been served by the Revs. Embry, Collins and Culverson. Its membership is about twenty-five. The early services were held in the schoolhouse, but later in a building donated to the society by Mrs. Davis.

THE BAPTIST CHURCH was organized June 26, 1881,

with seventeen members. Early services were held in the school-house, and later in a rented store room in town, but are now conducted in the courthouse. The society had occasional services by Revs. J. C. Posy and L. D. Robinson but had no regular pastor until the coming of Rev. J. M. Wood. The church membership is now seventy-six. A Sabbath School was started January 1, 1883 by Mr. James Elgin.

Benton Post, No. 61, G.A.R., was organized May 28, 1882, with twenty-four members, and the following officers: M. W. Halsey, C.: T. H. Stephens, S.V.C.: O. C. Howe, J.V.C.: G. M. Keller, Surgeon: E. D. Bowen, Quarter Master: A. H. Broadstone, O.D.; C. S. Matteson, O.G.: John Goggin, Adjt. The Post now numbers thirty-six and has the same officers except W. H. Mock, O.G., and J. A. DuBois, Adjt. Meetings are held on the second and fourth Saturdays of the month in the courthouse.

BANKING—The first bank established at Anthony was started in July, 1879, by P. Anderson, who began business in a small frame structure standing in the street. The stone building now in use was begun at once and pushed to completion at the cost of $2,500. The bank has a capital of $20,000.

GLOBE MILLS—These mills were built in 1880-81, and put in operation February 22, of the latter year, by Holdridge, Connelly & Co., the present owners. The mill building is of brown sandstone, 38 x 40, and has three stories and a basement. It is fitted with five run of buhr-stones, one set of rolls, and an engine of seventy horsepower. The capacity of the mill is 150 barrels of flour per day, and their total cost a trifle over $25,000. A large trade is had with all points in the Indian Territory, as well as with surrounding towns.

THE JOURNAL—The first number of the *Anthony Journal* appeared on August 22, 1878, as a five-column folio, and bore the name of J. S. Soule as editor and proprietor. On May 22, 1879, the paper passed into the hands of C. W. Greene, who ran it until April 8, 1881, when it was temporarily suspended. Meantime several changes had been made, the paper enlarging Aug. 15, 1879, to a six-column, and May 7, 1880 to a seven-column folio. In this latter shape it was resurrected October 27, 1881, by Fletcher Meredith. August 31, 1882, it was made a six-column quarto, and on March 1, 1883, the office was leased by B. F. Widner for one year. The paper has a circulation of 350 and a good advertising patronage.

THE REPUBLICAN—The *Anthony Republican* was started October 19, 1879, by Moffett and Metcalf. Its first appearance was as a six-column folio. This was changed January 8, 1880, to a seven-column, and December 23, 1882, to a six-column quarto. Metcalf's name disappears February 26, 1880, and that of George Moffett stands alone until May 27, of the same year when A. S. Lindsay became a partner in the business, which August 5, of the same year passed into his sole possession. The paper has circulation of 450.

HISTORY OF CHURCHES IN ANTHONY
(after 1883)

From "Historical Collection of Harper County Churches—1961"

Assembly of God (1951)

The church was organized in 1951 under the direction of Rev. Clyde Gilbert. The church was originally established in Corwin, but, because of a dwindling population, it was moved to Anthony. In 1952 the congregation moved into the present building, located at 408 N. Santa Fe. Present membership, 24.

Central Baptist Church (1936)

This church was organized in 1936 as the "Faith Fundamental Baptist Church" with thirty-two charter members. After meeting at various locations a permanent location was established at 535 S. Bluff, August 1942.

On January 4, 1945 the congregation voted to change the name to "Central Baptist Church."

At present the church is supporting nine missionaries in six countries, as well as the Baptist Bible College at Springfield, Mo. Present membership, 150.

The First Baptist Church

The early history of this church may be found on page 58.

In 1885 services were held in Union Hall over the Costa Hardware. On June 20, 1886, the new Baptist Church building was dedicated, the services were conducted by Rev. Harper of Wichita, Rev. Parker of Clearwater, and Rev. J. R. Edwards, local pastor.

On July 1, 1886, the new Baptistry was used for the first time. Rev. Edwards immersed Mrs. Bertie Kinsley, Minnie Ermin and Mrs. Smithson. Present membership, 170.

Christian Church (1880)

The early history of this church may be found on page 58.

The first church building was built in 1885 on south Bluff. A. L. Shelton, son of Mr. and Mrs. J. O. Shelton, became one of the Christian Church's greatest medical missionaries. In 1921, Dr. Shelton was killed by bandits in Tibet where he had spent many years as a missionary. The present church building was dedicated in 1913. At the present time there are 350 resident and 150 non-resident members.

(United) The First Methodist Church, Anthony

The early history of this church may be found on page 58.

In 1904 the original building was enlarged. In 1909 the present church was designed and built. A new Carnegie pipe organ was installed at this time. It is with a great deal of pride that the church members mention Miss Ruth Hoath who spent nearly forty years in India as a missionary under the Women's Board of the Methodist Church. Present membership, 500.

The Congregational Church, Anthony, 1879

The early history of this church may be found on page 58.

A new church was built and dedicated November 27, 1910. The stained glass windows, irreplacable by American craftsmen, are in memory of three members of the first church choir and other devoted workers. A storm severely damaged these windows. The choir window was replaced. Present membership, 80.

Church of Christ, Anthony (1942)

The Church of Christ was organized in the home of Mrs. Ansel Tower on November 2, 1942 with a membership of twelve. A permanent church home was completed and dedicated January 30, 1949 with Bill Thompson of Lufkin, Texas, the speaker. Present membership, 67.

The First Church of God, Anthony (1884)

The first services were held in the home of J. F. Prouse northwest of Anthony. People came to the Prouse home for services in wagons and on horseback. Later this group met in a schoolhouse west of the county farm. In 1906 a small church building was erected. A new and larger church was constructed and dedicated September 15, 1946. The present membership is 65.

The Anthony Church of God

This church is located on South Franklin. Regular services are held with Rev. Willie Murphy, Gutherie, Okla., conducting on alternate Sundays. The average attendance is 20.

The Church of the Nazarene (1929)

Following a meeting held by Rev. J. P. Wear in a rented store building in Anthony, February 1929, Church of the Nazarene was organized with eleven charter members. The present church building was built and dedicated March 21, 1937. Present membership, 50.

The Grace Episcopal Church, Anthony (1889)

The first services were conducted by the Rev. D. Howard of Arkansas City in 1889, in a store building on Main Street and later in the courthouse. The present church was built and consecrated on April 23, 1908, by the Rt. Rev. S. M. Griswold, Bishop of Salina. The beautiful stained glass windows were brought here from the old cathedral at Salina. Present membership, 35.

Sacred Heart Parish, Anthony (1879)

One of the earliest Church organizations in Anthony was the Catholic, which was organized in 1879. From that time until 1908, services were held in some of the more prominent homes, namely, Mrs. A. D. Kinsley, Mrs. Samuel P. Black, Mrs. Ernest Bosc and Mrs. Floyd Bassett. A small frame church building was constructed and dedicated April 28, 1908, by the Rt. Rev. Bishop J. J. Hennessey of Wichita. In October 1934, construction of the present parish rectory was begun, and completed in April of the following year. The present church was dedicated by the Rt. Rev. Bishop Aug. J. Schwertner, D.D., of Wichita on Nov. 1, 1938. Present membership, 175.

The House of Prayer, Anthony (1928)

The House of Prayer was organized by Elder C. J. McGanse in 1928. The permanent church home was in a church formerly owned by the Methodist Congregation. Small membership.

The *Anthony Republican* and The *Anthony Bulletin,* May 20, 1938.

ANTHONY HOSE TEAM WORLD CHAMPIONS
IN 1888 AND 1889

This was the proud claim of the city during the late '80's and involves a story that will always be a "standout" in the history of the city. Of the team that twice won the national title—in 1888, in Kansas City, and in 1889, in Denver—three are still living in Anthony. They are Harvey Davis, Frank Firestone and Thomas Fanning.

In those days the fire department was the pride and joy of the city, well equipped with new uniforms, and a feature of every parade and festival.

It was on June 5, 1888, that the men of Company no. 1, Anthony, entered the firemen's tournament in Wichita. The affair lasted three days, with the locals winning the first and third days and taking second honors on the second day.

The climax of a most successful year (1888) came on Sept. 13, when, in competition with the crack teams of the nation, in Kansas City, they emerged victorious.

Anthony hose team again jumped into prominence when, on Aug. 23, 1889, they successfully defended their championship in Colorado.

The team reached the "Mile High City" a week ahead of time and had time to get accustomed to the change of altitude before the contest began.

The first prize won was the amateur coupling contest in which Ed Herold and Thomas Fanning took first prize in 8 seconds, it being $50.00. Hart Hanlon took $10.00, third money in foot race. The team also took second money, $35.00, in the professional coupling contest. Following this, they annexed third money in the straight away race, $150.00.

Saturday, Aug. 24 was the "great day" for the locals. On this day occurred the championship event, which was a run of 400 feet and the laying of 200 feet of hose, dry, and this was completed in 30 1/5 seconds, making them for the second time, the champions of the nation, and the winners of $500.00. The same day Hart Hanlon took second money in the foot race, $50.00.

In all, $791.00 in prize money and the national championship was won by the Anthony team in the Denver tournament.

Members of the team were: Grant Travis, Harvey Davis, Len Sander, Will Bent, John Bickingham, George Ebbs, L. A. Sweetland, Tom Saunders, Will Allyn, Frank Firestone, Frank Garber, Lester Sanders, Harry Northrop, Ben Frasier, Chas. Cooper, Ed Herold, Chas. Hanselman, W. H. Jennings and Thomas Fanning.

To say that the team was enthusiastically welcomed home is putting it mildly. The town turned out en masse to welcome the victors. The train was met at the depot with an escort of honor and the members of the team, as they stepped from the train, were greeted with the enthusiastic cheers of the large crowd which was waiting.

Upon the platform was the Harper fire department headed by the Anthony Cornet band. The Knights of Pythias, in full uniform, saluted the victors as they filed passed to take their place in the forming parade.

Main Street was seething with activity that day. The fluttering bunting, the booming of cannons and the shouting of the crowds added to the general din, while later in the evening festive bonfires blazed in a dozen directions.

An elaborate banquet was given the champions their first evening home.

The *Anthony Republican* and the *Anthony Bulletin*
May 19, 1938

EARLY PHYSICIANS MET DIFFICULTIES

Dr. J. H. Callendar of Ripon, Wis., arrived Tuesday with six or seven wagon loads of lumber and household goods. Two of his sons came with him. We understand that Dr. Callendar had the lumber framed in Wisconsin all ready to put together and ship to Wichita.

Their claim was two and one half miles east of town. The original story-and-a-half house was constructed of white pine and shipped from Wisconsin to Wichita, and freighted to Anthony in wagons, still stands. In early days this home was considered almost a mansion.

Dr. J. H. Callendar was the first dentist in Harper County. There was not enough business here so he made regular trips to the surrounding towns of Caldwell, Belle Plaine, Wellington, Oxford, Attica and Harper.

Dr. C. J. Callendar is one of the aforementioned sons. He was a grown boy but not yet of age when he came here. He

The First House in Anthony, Kansas

Harper County Courthouse, Anthony, 1968

Early Anthony Main Street

Stagecoach leaving Glenn House (First frame building in Harper) 1880

Holmes Mercantile Store 1912, Bluff City

Wood cut of Attica Art Gallery - by Ted Young

Photograph Exhibit: Face, painting; hooked rugs, designed and made by Agnes Nye; sculpture by Bill Nye.

Montage of Photographs of Harper County Art—Clockwise: "Runnymede," Agnes Nye; "Country Road," Agnes Nye; "Sunflowers," Fern Crow; "Oil Well," Dorothy Scarlett; "Wheatfields," Peg Charles; "Elevator, Bluff City," Connie Williams; and center, Carol Long with her "Poppies."

Fair Grounds 1910

Charles Corothers, Anthony, Kansas

helped his father on their claim, then he took a claim himself, bought and sold several quarters of land and made enough money thereby to put himself through four years of medical school at the University of New York, from which he graduated in the spring of 1888.

He came immediately to Anthony to practice medicine, married Miss Mary Kate Wright, daughter of the first groceryman in Anthony.

In later years, upon being asked, Dr. Callendar told of some of his experiences through the years. "Dr. Bowers and I performed emergency operations on kitchen tables." He says now that we would be put in jail today for such a thing. "The remarkable thing was that most of them got well. On one occasion the family was so poor that they did not own a table of any kind, so Dr. Bowers and I laid the sick boy down on the floor, getting on our knees we performed an operation on him for an abcess of the liver. The boy recovered. A few years later while standing on the streets of Anthony, someone poked me in the back and said, 'Hey, Doc, do you know me?' It was this same boy that we had operated on."

Anthony Republican, May 20, 1948, Notes.

RECOLLECTIONS OF PIONEER LIFE

Robert D. Hilts is one of the oldest residents of Anthony living at this time. He was born in 1885, in Springdale, Hamilton County, Ohio, which is now Cincinnati. He was 93 years old January 27, 1948, and came to Anthony in February, 1884, with his family, which at that time was a wife and three children, Laura Hilts (Hacker), Bessie Hilts (Limbird), and Russel Hilts. Eight children were born in Kansas. Glen, Lottie (deceased), Mary Hilts (Harlan), Robert, Cecil, Helen Hilts (Getterman), Mildred Hilts (Schmitz), and Durland.

In the spring of 1885 Mr. Hilts took his family to Meade County, Kansas, and settled on a claim. Mr. Hilts said, "As a pioneer of the Kansas prairies we had to endure many hardships. We lost one child in Meade County because there was no doctor available. We lived in a dugout with a box building at one end in which the family slept. The house was pretty comfortable for a prairie home but I remember January 7, 1886, we had a blizzard and after it ended we took five tubs of snow from the bedroom.

"I raised the first wheat in Meade County, and owned the first binder.

"I brought my family back to Anthony in the fall of 1894. We came back in a covered wagon and camped along the way at night. The trip took four or five days. We followed township lines, cutting across the country as much as possible. We had a blizzard on the way and had to hold quilts at the end of the covered wagon to keep out the snow so the children could sleep. We camped west of Attica one night of the trip. We went into Attica the next morning and ordered breakfast about nine-thirty. It was noon before we got it due to the blizzard the night before. We just called it dinner and started for Anthony. We arrived in Anthony about sundown. I had to go to the hardware store to get some stove pipe to put up our stove in the house I had already rented.

"After coming to Anthony I worked at excavating, moving buildings, hauling sand from Bluff Creek, and I moved the old Congregational church to the ally and dug the basement for the present church.

"The coldest spell I remember here in Anthony was the winter of 1898. It was twenty degrees below zero. We hauled blocks of ice from the Treadwell ranch north of Anthony to Arnett's ice house, which was located about where the Farmer Co-op is now located. The blocks of ice were fourteen inches thick. I also remember hauling a load of oats from sixteen miles southwest of Anthony. The snow was so deep that I had to detour several miles out of the way."

Mr. Hilts rode in the sixtieth anniversary parade. He wore his wedding suit which had a Prince Albert coat of broadcloth. He hopes to ride a horse in the seventieth celebration.

Mrs. Hilts was killed in an automobile accident between Anthony and Harper in 1930.

The *Anthony Republican,* June 11, 1881

BITTEN BY SNAKE

A little son of Alvin Vangilder was bitten on the ankle by a large rattlesnake last Sunday afternoon about dark.

His father administered whiskey and kept his son under the influence of it for several days, also applying a cud of tobacco to the wound. The limb swelled as far as the hip, but yielded to the treatment and the little fellow is now all right again.

Parents should be very careful at this season of the year to caution their children not to play in the prairie grass, and always to keep a sharp lookout for snakes of which there seems to be an unusually large number lately.

FARMER COWBOY FOOTRACE STORY

Asbury Mock, if pressed, will tell you many an interesting story of early incidents in Anthony. In those days, Mr. Mock lived out on Bluff Creek west of Anthony and he went barefoot for so many years his feet became calloused to a degree that sandburs had no terror for him. The other party to the story was Anderson Hilton, a two-gun cowboy and good-natured puncher, who figured largely in early history.

Mr. Mock came to town one day and challenged Hilton to a footrace, distance a half mile. Hilton was quick to accept the challenge and it was agreed that the challenger had the right to name the place and conditions.

After Mr. Mock stipulated that the race should be run barefooted with trousers rolled to the knees and the track should be along the bank of Bluff Creek.

When these conditions were made known to the cowboy he said, "Come on boys, it's on me; I couldn't run ten feet with my boots off."

The early-day "thirst parlors" took in ten dollars extra that day, and nobody was killed.

Anthony Republican, May 20, 1948

Thomas Fanning is the only living member of the Champion Fire Hose Team who won a World's Championship in Denver, Colo., in 1889. He served with the local fire company for 60 years. Mr. Fanning, who will be 89 years old this summer, lives at 324 N. Jennings, where his grandson Tommy is also making his home.

First railroad in Anthony—St. Louis, Fort Scott, and Wichita. May 13, 1885.

Monday, June 25, 1888, the Frisco was completed into Anthony.

Omaha, Hutchinson, and Gulf railway first train to serve Anthony was June 3, 1890.

The Choctaw Northern Railroad opened its line to Anthony Dec. 31, 1900.

The Orient line started laying tracks for its line May 10, 1902.

Anthony Free Press, June 30, 1887

BRICKYARD EARLY INDUSTRY

Through the courtesy of Thomas Fanning we enjoyed a pleasant ride Monday to the brickyard of Wilson & Fanning, on Spring Creek, and were shown around over the immense institution of manufacturing industry. This enterprising firm employs a force of twenty-five or thirty men who are kept busy moulding and burning brick to supply the demand now required for the construction of the numerous buildings in course of construction. They are now burning a kiln which contains about three hundred and fifty thousand bricks which will be finished and ready for use by the first of next week, which in addition to the quantity already burned which make about five hundred thousand bricks now on hand all of which are sold and then barely enough to supply the demand. Messers Wilson and Fanning have been to a heavy expense this spring in getting their yard in excellent and convenient condition. It covers a space of about four acres besides the numerous drying houses cooking and sleeping apartments, etc., and their expenses amount to five hundred dollars every month, all of which is paid out and circulated in our city. A ride out to this yard and to witness the busy scene that takes place there daily in making material, which is the finest that has been made in this part of the state for the buildings now being erected is proof enough of Anthony's enormous building boom and also of the enterprise and push of Messers Wilson and Fanning.

The *Anthony Republican* and the *Anthony Bulletin* May 19, 1938

HUNDREDS WILL SEE PLANE STOP

History will be written at 1:35 o'clock this afternoon when a special U.S. airmail plane stops at the municipal airport for a pouch of mail—the first local airmail stop in the history of the city.

The stop is in connection with the observation of National

Airmail week, and hundreds of persons from all over the country
will view the pick-up. Harry Gains, well-known Wichita aviator,
will pilot the plane to Anthony.

New Post Office Building Completed This Year

The new Anthony post office building was dedicated on Feb.
15, 1938, a date which symbolized the end of one era and the
beginning of another, and strengthened the faith of local citizens in the future stability and growth of Anthony. Construction of the new building ended a period during which the
Anthony post office moved about "from pillar to post."

The new edifice, representing an expenditure of nearly $63,000,
evidences the federal government's faith in Anthony's perma-
nence as an important trading center for a large territory, and
anticipates the healthy growth of this community beyond that
achieved in the past.

Anthony Republican and the *Anthony Bulletin,* May 20, 1948

Sugar Mill Early Industry

An early-day industry, one of the many financed in the early
eighties by the businessmen of Anthony, was a sugar mill, the
installation of which is described by the *Republican,* in its issue
of Oct. 6, 1905, as follows:

"In 1879 the department of agriculture at Washington was
stirring the hope of the western farmers over the possibilities of
making sugar from common cane. A big experiment plant was
put in at Fort Scott, and the government spent at least $100,000
trying to make merchantable sugar there. They made sugar,
lots of it, but it was coarse and strong, and cost more to make
than it would sell for.

"Anthony had the fever, too. The businessmen chipped in
and built a $10,000 sugar mill northwest of the Santa Fe depot.
It was a fine layout of engines, crushers, granulators, purifying,
and other tanks, and a centrifugal dryer. The cane was crushed
so dry that it was used as a fuel under the boilers and evaporating pans, mixed with a little prairie hay. The first year they
made only a fair quality of syrup. A. Markwell studied the
sugar question all summer; when cane ripened he announced
that he would make sugar by the new government process. So
one Saturday, Judge A. R. Blackburn sent to his farm a couple

of big loads of early amber cane, the first ripe, to be crushed in Mr. Markwell's horsepower mill and used for an experiment. The writer, with the Markwell boys, Asbury, Elmar and James, and their pretty red-headed sister Addie, kept poking prairie hay under the evaporating pans until 10:00 o'clock Saturday night, when a fine, thick syrup was secured, with no trace of sugar to show for the chemicals Mr. Markwell had stirred in during the cooking. We slept with the Markwell boys that night and the next morning all hurried out to the pans to see if the syrup had crystallized. There was not a trace of sugar, just a thick, fine-flavored amber syrup. Later, Mr. Markwell dipped out a tin can full and took it to the home of Judge Blackburn to show. He explained how he had followed exactly the government formula, and could not account for the failure to get results. While they were discussing the matter, Mr. Markwell kept idly stirring the syrup in the can with a stick, holding it up and letting the syrup drip back into the can. Some sugar crystals formed and in a half hour the can was so thick with sugar that it could not be stirred. All it needed to start granulation was the stirring. There was great excitement in town that Sunday morning, and although Mr. Markwell was a deeply religious man, he forgot to go to church. The sugar mill made several hundred barrels of sugar that year, but it could not be produced profitably, so the hole in the back of the draw where the mill was located is all that is left of the enterprise."

The *Anthony Republican*, May 20, 1948

GENERATION OF 1897 HAD ROUDY YOUNGUNS

Long before Sweet Adeline became the much abused favorite of all inebriated vocalists, the same yearning for convivial melody must have possessed the minds of those who had looked too long upon the wine when it was red. When the early-day residents of Anthony had been successful (presumably) in stopping that sort of thing, another problem arose. The editor of the *Republican,* in the issue of October 1, 1897, labels it "A terrible vice of the younger generation," and has this comment to make:

"The old-time rowdies of this city long ago learned that it was greatly to their disadvantage to prowl around at night and disturb the respectable citizens by singing ribald selections.

"More recently, however, they have been succeeded by members of a younger gang, about 16 years of age, who meet at a specified place, go out late in the evening, and burlesque the song, "There'll Be a Hot Time in the Old Town Tonite." Apparently this is the only song the boys are familiar with, since they sing it over and over again, and repeat it some more.

"If the parents of these young and irresponsible schoolboys would keep them at home at nights, where they belong, or if the police would provide them with a night's lodging, it would do a great deal toward elevating the younger generation. Furthermore, people who desire a full night's sleep would not be disturbed by the moonlight chorus."

The *Anthony Republican*
May 20, 1948.

First Autos Were a Nuisance

Anthony editors apparently thought very little of the future of the automombile in the early nineteen hundreds, since no reference could be found in the newspapers' files relative to the first purchase of a car, either in Anthony or Harper County.

The first item located was published in the April 7, 1905 issue of the *Republican* and reads as follows:

"Automobiles are becoming numerous; it may soon be necessary for the council to set a speed limit if horse owners are not to be imposed on and hope to keep in sight of the machines. P. G. Walton has a big Haynes-Apperson machine; E. C. Wilcox a Ford equally large; M. L. Dickson has the most used of any an Oldsmobile; while Dr. Updegraff and Charles Rutherford fly around in Toledos. Cashier Sam L. Smith is figuring on a machine, and W. E. Treadwell will have a powerful machine of his own make in a few days. Mr. Treadwell designed his own auto after visiting the famous Madison Square Garden's show more than a year ago, taking the very best features of the 150 machines on exhibition at that time. He has embodied these features into a machine that should prove to be the best and safest touring car ever made, in the opinion of expert machine men who have been permitted to see the machine he has designed. As he has built the auto for pastime, being fond of the pleasures of mechanical construction, Mr. Treadwell has taken his time and has fitted it up, both inside and out, in first-class style."

Another item, this time in the *Bulletin,* early in the spring of the same year, voices the complaint of a country subscriber to the effect that automobiles were proving themselves to be nothing more than "noisy nuisances," and elaborated the assertion that a carelessly driven machine almost scared a team of horses out of its wits as it went snorting along the road west of Anthony.

The *Anthony Republican* and the *Anthony Bulletin*
May 20, 1948

Wholesale Grocery Organized Here in 1902

No other concern in this city has been more closely connected with the changing fortunes of Anthony and southwest Kansas during the last past century than the Anthony Wholesale Grocery company.

In 1902, when it was first organized, its founders faced adverse comment and the prediction that the new venture would "land on the rocks" within a short time. But because these men, and those who followed them, believed sincerely in the future of Anthony and surrounding territory, and because from the first the concern was run according to principles which were fundamentally sound, the new firm thrived and prospered and has continued to do so during the forty-six years which followed.

Adopting the slogan, "Service and Quality," the company has its own brands of "King Parrot and Farm King," brands of food, which are well and favorably known throughout a wide territory.

When it was organized in 1902, the company had a capital of $40,000. The present capital, $200,000, is a partial indication of the steady increase in the value of business done by the concern, which before the depression reached a maximum of a million and a half dollars a year, for several different years.

Following the program of expansion, as the business grew and prospered, two branch houses were established—at Alva in 1910, and at Fairview in 1925.

The *Anthony Republican* and the *Anthony Bulletin*
May 20, 1948

Ranny-Davis Co. Early Organization

The Ranny-Davis Mercantile Co. opened for business in

1903 in the two rooms east of their present location.

In 1904 Mr. Sloop built the building now occupied.

Mr. J. B. Randels, father of Stan Randles, was the first branch manager, the others being J. C. Verser, C. F. Rutherford, A. A. Granger, M. H. Hoyt and Geo. Kane.

Nearly all of the food sold when they first started was in bulk. About the only canned food items were corn and tomatoes, some of the items handled were sugar, black-strap molasses and flour in the barrels.

Oatmeal, also packed in barrels, was the only cereal. Dried fruits sold in 50 pound cotton sacks. Rice in 226 pound bags, was imported from Japan, none then being grown in this country.

Stovepipe, coal buckets, wooden tubs and buckets, tinware and galvanized ware were big sellers. Axle grease was a demand item.

Buggy whips, currycombs and brushes, and other articles associated with the horse-and-buggy age were a part of a wholesale grocery stock.

In those days we sold meat, which was corded like wood by the carload. There were salt sides, bellies, smoked sides, backs and hams. Matches were of the old-time sulphur type, followed by those which exploded with a bang and startled housewives out of their wits.

Teas were packed in quarter and half chests and spices were packed in six and ten pound boxes. Crackers, too, were boxed at about 23 pounds to the box.

Cigars and stogies for smokers and chewing tobacco were in plentiful supply, but there were no ready-made cigarettes. The only wrapping paper was straw paper in bundles. Roll paper was unknown.

About 700 items were listed in the Ranny-Davis cost book in the early 1900. Now the number is approximately 4,000.

We feature the three brands which were: Ranny's Finest, Santa Fe and Pan Tree.

THE ANTHONY SALT INDUSTRY

Salt was discovered in the area in 1887 while an oil and gas well was being drilled near Hutchinson. That same year Anthony salt was discovered.

A salt plant was started by a Mr. Mulke but due to poor management it was closed to be reopened by P. G. Walton.

The first salt wells were pumped from 1,050 feet but did not produce enough natural brine so water was pumped into the wells and was repumped.

The brine was placed in low vats for evaporation by heat from below the vats. For years the rakes or skips which worked the brine to keep the settling salt from burning, were manually manipulated. In later years the rakes were electrically driven.

The plant produced 50 tons of salt per day which were sent all over the world.

Different grades of salt were produced. Block salt was made by placing in a hydraulic press. Table and flour salt were products of the plant. Flour salt was rolled extremely fine to be used in cake and pancake mixes.

The salt works was first known as the Anthony Salt Company, later, the Orient Salt Company and last as the Globe Salt Company.

The plant operated until 1936; at that time Carey Salt of Hutchinson bought the enterprise and the Anthony salt operation came to an end.

ANTHONY SALT PLANT

From *The Anthony Republican,* January 3, 1896.

The Anthony Salt Plant has been sold at Sheriff's sale for $4,000.00. This is the plant in which the City of Anthony invested $23,000.00 a few years ago.

The *Anthony Republican* and the *Anthony Bulletin*
May 19, 1938

So shrieked the headline in the Oct. 6, 1905 issue of the *Republican,* the item describing the disintegration being as follows:

"The city of Anthony voted bonds in 1880 to build a city building, which was turned over to the county for a courthouse. Homemade brick and the native soft, red sandstone were used for its construction. Time and the elements have disintegrated the brick and mortar and stone; and the building is slowly but surely crumbling away. For some years cracks have been developing in the walls, growing steadily in number and in size.

Officials in the courthouse have frequently expressed fear as to the safety of the building, particularly in case of a high wind.

The commissioners secured a building engineer to inspect the building, and he pronounced it to be highly unsafe.

At a special election, held May 21, 1907, the voters of the county approved the issuance of bonds for a new building. Excavation work and the laying of the foundation was started in the fall of the same year. The cornerstone was laid Jan. 29, 1908.

The *Anthony Republican* and the *Anthony Bulletin*
May 20, 1948

ANTHONY LIBRARY DONATED BY GROUP FROM NEW YORK

No story about the history of Anthony would be complete without paying a tribute to the founders of the Anthony Free Public Library and reading room, one of the city's oldest civic institutions.

The question of establishing and maintaining a free public library and reading room was brought before the mayor and council of the city of Anthony in February 1897, by a petition signed by more than 50 taxpayers.

The mayor and council were informed that William B. Jones and William K. Palmer, both of New York City, had delivered, free of all charge, to B. H. Stedman of Anthony, more than five hundred books, suitable for such a library.

Whereupon the council ordered that the question of establishing and maintaining a free library and reading room be submitted to the qualified electors of the city at the annual municipal election held on April 6, 1897. The council formally declared the proposition carried April 9, 1897.

The state laws require the affairs of a public library to be in charge of a library board of twelve residents of the city, and the mayor. Mayor John D. Brown by and with the consent and approval of the council appointed the following to constitute the first library board, May 10, 1897: Mrs. Elizabeth Childs, Mrs. Philura A. Olmstead, Mrs. Leille C. Noftzger, Mrs. Lulu Carrithers, Miss Jennie Davy, Miss Stella Painter, Miss Sarah Hurd, Rev. John R. Edwards, John W. Clendenin, W. E. Blackburn, C. A. Poorman and T. H. McDowell.

W. E. Blackburn, then editor of the Anthony *Republican,* was elected president of the board in 1903 and held that office until 1912. During that period, in 1909, an architect was hired and plans were accepted to begin work on the new library building (at the present site) and the building was dedicated in 1910 as a memorial to Andrew Carnegie, donor of the funds to erect the edifice.

The *Anthony Journal*, Aug. 22, 1878

Town and Country

Come all ye weary and heavy laden, tax-payers of the east, and Harper County will give you rest.

*   *   *   *

We will send one copy of the *Journal* six months to the party who will furnish us the largest watermelon of the season.

*   *   *   *

Never in our lives have we seen or heard of such a rush for any county, as the one that is being made to this county at the present time.

*   *   *   *

Boarding by the week can be had here as cheap as in our neighboring towns on the east and north. Wichita not excepted. Good meals can be had at $3.50 per week.

*   *   *   *

The road between here and Wichita is completely lined with freighters and emigrants, freighting for and moving to the beautiful city of Anthony and its surrounding country.

*   *   *   *

We challenge any town in the state to show a better public well than the one at Anthony. It is located in the center of the crossing of the two principal business streets, and furnishes hundreds of gallons of the pure and sparkling beverage to both man and beast.

*   *   *   *

A herd of sixteen wild horses was seen about seven miles west of town last week. A man living near El Dorado, Butler County, captured a beautiful little colt, and started home rejoicing. It is a common thing to see herds of these beautiful steeds on our prairies.

*   *   *   *

We understand that the wheat buyers of Wichita say that the best wheat brought to that market, so far, came from Harper County. You, that lived in the alkali district, please "Put that in your pipe and smoke it."

*   *   *   *

The town company has put a heavy chain around the public well, in a circle, within sufficient distance to keep the immense amount of teams that are watered there daily from making it muddy and disagreeable.

*   *   *   *

Mr. Brokaw surprised us last Saturday, by bringing into our office a watermelon, something less than a flour barrel. It weighed a little over 34 pounds; and about a dozen of our numerous friends, who helped us get away with it pronounced it excellent. We understand that Mr. B. has had them still larger. They are grown on the sod.

The *Anthony Republican* and the *Anthony Bulletin*
May 20, 1948

MUNICIPAL LAKE NOTED BEAUTY SPOT

The Anthony Municipal Lake project was started in the fall of 1934, and was a government and city project. The Government furnished $80,000 and the City appropriated $24,300. The lake was completed in May of 1935, and filled to overflowing with the first rain shortly after its completion.

The project was known as the Spring Creek Reservoir and Water Works Improvement. The lake was begun and completed under the administration of Mayor M. D. Hoopes and Edgar C. Miller and L. C. Boscas, commissioners. The lake covered 152 acres with water and the lake and park total 410 acres.

The whole park area includes a golf course, cabins, shelter houses, gun club, Boy Scout cabin, and the lake in which fishing and boating are enjoyed by thousands yearly. The drainage area for the lake itself is 24 square miles of land. Originally over 10,000 trees were planted to make this property one of the beauty spots in southern Kansas.

ANTHONY HOUSING PROJECT

On July 1, 1966, a survey was started for a low rent housing project for the city of Anthony.

A five man commission was chosen with Earl Kropp as chairman, other members of the committee were: Clarence Hoopes, Roger Andrews, Bill Bayless and Paul Shannon.

After a great deal of work and study a loan was secured June 2, 1967, for 46 units. Forty will be for elderly people and will include 36 one-bedroom, 7 two-bedroom and 3 three-bedroom units.

A combination recreation center will have kitchen facilities and dining space for 90 people.

Some features of the project will be garbage collection and off-street parking. Their will be master TV antennas.

Ed Jones has been selected as executive director.

The landscaping will include 21 trees and 200 shrubs.

The rental minimum will start at $30.00 per month.

One may rent from this housing project after reaching 62 years of age.

Anthony

THE CITIZENS NATIONAL BANK

The first bank in Anthony was started in July 1879, by Philander Anderson. The bank was housed in a red stone building where the Citizens National bank is now located. The bank was called the Harper County Bank. On January 1, 1897, the business was taken over by the Anthony State Bank which was organized with a capital stock of $5,000. In 1903 the Anthony State Bank was succeeded by the newly organized Citizens National Bank with a capital stock of $50,000, which was increased to $100,000 on January 1, 1920. In 1948 the total assets of the bank were $5,100, 810.41. The total assets of the bank in 1953 were $5,344,213.18. According to the condensed statement at the close of business, March 31, 1968, the total assets were $7,316,702.15. The present officers are Charles Massner, President; J. H. Schnackenberg, Vice-President; Richard Bird, Cashier; Lucylle Snyder, Assistant Cashier. Directors: Dr. H. L. Galloway, Edgar C. Miller, Howard W. Hadsall, Rodney P. Olmstead and Kenneth Dusenbury.

THE FIRST NATIONAL BANK OF ANTHONY

Incorporated in 1885, the First National Bank of Anthony is now the oldest bank in Harper County, operating continuously under one charter and one name. On October 1, 1885, the total assets were $72,097.29. The original incorporators were Tilman H. Stephens, Geo. D. Thompson, Lyman A. Walton, O. F. Casteen, S. A. Darrough and D. F. Shooly.

The bank was started with a capital of $50,000.00. In 1886 this figure was increased to $100,000.00. Then came the financial stringency of 1893, when the Cherokee Outlet was opened, and Anthony, and Harper County lost heavily in population, the county losing 45 percent and the city of Anthony over 65 percent. It was at this crisis in the affairs of the institution that P. G. Walton was chosen cashier. He determined that no customer should suffer loss and induced the directors to consent to charge off $50,000.00 worth of paper made by people who had moved into the outlet and reorganized the bank on the basis of $50,000.00 capital.

Innumerable changes have come, and businesses have come and gone. The life of this bank covers a span of three wars, several economic depressions, including the closing of all banks in 1933, and covers an almost complete change in methods of agriculture, business and living conditions.

On March 4, 1935, the assets were $406,626.33, May 4, 1953 shows a figure of $2,557,051.05. The condensed statement at the close of business April 18, 1968 shows the assets to be $5,713,849.44.

The present officers are Kenneth E. Briggs, President; H. H. Halbower, Chairman of the Board; A. L. Griesinger, Vice-President and Cashier; Larry J. Lanie, Assistant Cashier.

Lyle C. Harris, C. D. Williams, Jr., M. L. Holaday are members of the board.

ANTHONY SCHOOL SYSTEM

From *The Anthony Republican*, May 20, 1948

Education has always been a factor of paramount importance in the community life of Anthony since the origin of the city seventy years ago. Romance and pathos have both been written into the history of the schools. The public school system was inaugurated May 1, 1879, with the engagement of Misses Clara Sherwood and Sarah Bidwell as teachers. Mr. G. H. Woodward was the first principal.

A school building was completed in July 1879, at a cost of $1,300.00. In the summer of 1882, two large wings were added at a cost of $1,300.00. Funds for both these outlays were secured by the issuance of district bonds, which were sold to the secretary of state at par.

In the fall of 1885 the city voted bonds totaling nearly $30,000.00 for the erection of a new building (old Washington school). Construction was started immediately.

On Sunday night, April 19, 1886, while the Washington school was being built, a mob of fifty men took charge of the edifice and proceeded to shoot the three Weaver boys for their attempted murder of Dell Shearer, a well-known cowboy living near Danville. This is the only instance of a lynching in the annals of Harper County history.

The members of the first high school graduating class were Miss Libbie Randels, Estella M. Halsey, Grace Russel and Frank C. Firestone. The graduation exercises were held in the old opera house, June 1, 1888.

On August 4, 1888, the Washington school was struck by lightning and burned to the ground, only a few records were saved, including the copper box that had been placed in the cornerstone by the first graduating class.

The school board immediately issued bonds for the erection of a new building.

Normal training was added to the high school curriculum in 1910. Home economics was an addition in 1915, and attracted an enrollment of seventy-five girls in its first year. A school nurse was employed by the board of education in 1921.

The local high school was admitted to the North Central Association of secondary schools and colleges in 1923.

In the spring of 1904, athletics was introduced into the Anthony High School, when a definite organization called the "Anthony High School Athletic Association" was formed.

The Anthony relays, held annually, has become the outstanding high school event of the year. Beginning in 1921, the meet has grown to the extent that it now attracts over 1,000 athletes. The "Queen of the Relays" became a feature of the meet in 1937, with Ruby Roach being elected as the first queen.

The present high school was built and dedicated January 7, 1921.

PRESENT DAY ANTHONY

Population of city—2,944

Anthony Schools: Washington Elementary, grades 1 through

4, 244 students, 12 teachers. Lincoln Elementary, grades 5 through 8, 205 students, 12 teachers. Anthony High School, 295 students, 21 teachers.

Number of books in the elementary school libraries—5,068.

Number of books in the high school libraries—4,126.

Number of books in the public library—8,941.

The Anthony Post Office is located at 121 W. Steadman. The Post Office was built in 1937. There are two R.F.D.'s operating from this office.

Lodges: A.F. & A.M. #200, Eastern Star, Odd Fellows, Rebekahs, American Legion, Veterans of Foreign Wars and American Legion Aux.

Civic Organizations: Kiwanis Club, Lions Club, Business and Professional Women's Club, Jaycees and Chamber of Commerce.

There are 13 churches in Anthony.

AIRPORT

Rated as the number one sod landing field in Kansas, the municipally owned Anthony Airport is located two miles west of town. With an elevation of 1,340 feet, two runways and a lighted field, the facility is equipped to handle all planes through a DC-3. A full-time attendant has charter service available, and top-rated hanger houses planes for local flying patrons. Mild temperatures make year-round flying available.

ANTHONY MUNICIPAL LAKE AND GOLF COURSE

Recreation can be found in abundance at the Anthony Lake and golf course, located just one and one-half miles from the city limits. The 152 acre lake offers fishing, boating and water-skiing for local enthusiasts, and the 258 acre park area provides a haven for campers and hikers. With one of the most attractive trailer parks in southern Kansas, the lake is fast becoming a favorite site for weekend visitors. The park area includes cabins, shelter houses, a gun club and a Boy Scout cabin. Anthony's scenic golf course, overlooking the lake, offers nine holes of pleasure and challenge on sand greens.

REST HOMES

Anthony has two rest homes, one located adjacent to the hospital, with a 50-bed capacity, and another located two blocks from Main Street, with an 18-bed capacity.

CITY HALL

Constructed in 1962, Anthony's all-modern City Building houses City Officials, the Police Department, and the Fire Department. Four fire trucks stand ready to protect the Anthony area, and firemen are on 24-hour call. Four full-time police officers patrol Anthony's residential and business district, and the Police Department is bolstered by a 20-man Auxiliary Police Force.

MUNICIPALLY OWNED POWER PLANT

Valued at over $2,000,000.00, the Anthony power plant provides the city and surrounding community with 5,250 kilowatts in generating capacity. Located two miles south of the city limits, the plant has a full staff of competent, highly trained men who operate at peak efficiency. Over 400 miles of rural lines are serviced by the plant. A reliable source of gas is available through Western Power & Gas Company, Inc.

ANTHONY HOSPITAL AND CLINIC

Independently self-supporting, Anthony's modern Community Hospital and Clinic was completed in 1961. An addition was completed in 1967, bringing the bed capacity to 54. The unit has a self-contained auxiliary power plant, and the Hospital is certified for Medicare. With a certified pharmacy, the hospital is completely modern. The clinic, while in the same building, is separate, and is staffed by competent doctors and nurses.

HOSPITAL HOLDS ANNUAL MEETING

From "The *Anthony Republican*," May 9, 1968

The ninth annual meeting of the Anthony Hospital and Clinic Association was held May 3 at the Commissioner's room at City Hall. James Chism was elected chairman, C. D. Williams, Jr., vice-chairman, and Vernon Bean, secretary.

ANTHONY DOWNS

Kansas' oldest race meet is held each July at the Anthony Downs, with five days of horse and dog races for the public. Officially instigated in 1904, the race meet has grown each year to its present capacity. Horses and dogs from throughout the United States are entered each year, and the grandstand at Anthony Downs holds a capacity crowd of 5,000. Due to the mild temperatures and fine accommodations, the one-half mile track teems with activity throughout the winter months as owners train their horses for summer races. The turf at the Anthony track never freezes, and as many as 60 persons are employed here during the winter. Paint horse races are held each Labor Day at Anthony Downs.

ANTHONY GETS GRANT FOR PARK

From "The *Wichita Eagle,*" August 29, 1967

Washington (AP)—A Bureau of Outdoor Recreation grant for a Kansas park was announced Monday.

Anthony received $4,845.00 to help acquire 8.8 acres.

Attica

HISTORY OF ATTICA, KANSAS

Written, 1932, and Revised, April 1949
By May Williamson

The *Attica Independent,* July 7, 1949

The little city of Attica, Kansas, is located near the central southern border of the state, in Harper County, and is about seventeen miles from the Oklahoma state line. Attica likely owes its existence to the fact that the land it occupies was the most convenient point for junction of the two railway lines of the Atchison, Topeka and Santa Fe Railroad, with the main line passing through Attica, going southwest and extending through Texas, New Mexico, and up the west coast of the United States. The other is a branch of the main line, which goes west to Medicine Lodge and Belvidere, Kansas.

In the latter part of June, 1884, Colonel W. G. Dickenson, General Agent for "The Arkansas Valley Town Company" purchased, for the company, the land which now comprises the present site of Attica.

This land was a part of what was known as "The Osage Trust Land." The Government held this land in trust for the Osage Tribe and provided by law that settlers might pre-empt it in tracts of 160 acres, paying $1.25 per acre. This money was placed in a fund for the Indians.

Miss Luzenie C. Walker pre-empted the quarter section of land on which the main part of Attica now stands, while the west part of Attica the town company purchased from Richard (Dick) Bodkin and his daughter, Mrs. Athelton, who like Miss Walker had pre-empted the land from the government.

The name of Attica was originally given to a post office that was located southeast of the present Attica on a farm known to us as the E. L. Thomas farm, but was pre-empted by I. L. Beeson, but the post office was soon moved to the G. H. Harkham farm. When the new town of Attica was started, it was agreed that the Post Office of Attica be moved to the new townsite and the town be called Attica.

Alden Speare made a plat of Attica in 1884, and its was placed on record at the County Seat at Anthony, July 9, 1884. (There is some question as to this date, as there was a survey of the town in July 1885.)

The first business transaction in the new town was said to have been the selling of $1,300.00 worth of lots to C. F. Meigs, of Harper County. The transaction was said to have been made in a buggy on Main Street, two blocks south of the depot.

Attica was a real boom town, for it grew up almost overnight. Within ninety days, the original townsite was sold out and a new addition was put on the market. The lumber for the first building was hauled from Harper by an ox team. The building was built by J. E. Hamilton in July, 1884, and was where the Tredenick business building now stands. He established the first grocery and general store in town. Another of the early buildings was a hotel which was known as the National Hotel and was where the Champlin service station now stands.

The coming of the railroad was a memorable event for the citizens of the town and nearby county, for Miss Luzenie C. Walker, commonly known as "The Old Maid Walker," who had pre-empted the land on which the southeast part of Attica is

built, refused to accept the price that the condemnation committee had named for the corner of her land over which the new
A.T. & S.F. Railroad was to be laid.

Miss Walker appealed to the District Court to allow her
more money for the land. This would have meant a great delay
in the building of the railroad into town, but after all, the material and equipment had been collected at the very edge of Miss
Walker's land, the citizens and workmen, under the management
of a certain stranger who happened in town, started working
on Sunday morning at one o'clock laying the track across Miss
Walker's land and on into town. By doing this work on Sunday
it was impossible for Miss Walker to secure an injunction against
the railroad company to stop the work. In this way, the track
was laid and an A.T. & S.F. railroad engine steamed into town
before night. The town and country was at white heat over the
event, and real frontier celebration ensued.

For a long time, Attica was the terminus of the Atchison,
Topeka, and Santa Fe Railway Company. The population increased by leaps and bounds. People from every class and walk
of life poured into town, buildings were erected in a few days or
a few weeks time at most. Many buildings were made of planks
stood on end, many were indeed crude affairs, but hotels and
eating places were in such demand that any kind of housing was
acceptable. There were no city officials or organization, and rev-
elry prevailed. A bad man by the name of Dave Sharp, from
Caldwell, Kansas, took over the city and ruled for twenty-four
hours. After this ordeal, it was decided the town should be
incorporated.

On Feb. 16, 1885, a petition was presented to the County
Commissioners, and Sam Wolf was appointed census taker.
There were then about 1,500 people in town.

An election was called, and J. T. Bodkin was elected the first
Mayor of Attica. Beesson was elected Police Judge. The town
made improvements and carried on all its business and expenses
from fines collected, and without a cent of tax of any kind.

The business section of the town, as well as the residential
section, grew rapidly. Some of the buildings were brick structures
and were more permanent than the earlier ones.

Two doctors, known as the Elrick Brothers, established the
first drugstore. L. A. Jones had a blacksmith shop where the
Charley Evans Machine Shop now stands. C. E. Voorees and

C. W. Insley owned the first hardware store. The first postmaster was Pete Schleppy, who was a fine, intelligent man, but was a hunchback. (According to the State Historical records of Post Offices, Virgil J. Beesson was the first postmaster of Attica. This was probably the early post office which was located south of the present Attica.) (Sanders.) The location of the first post office was said to have been in a frame building where the brick Ballard building now stands, on the west side of Main Street.

C. L. (Curg) Beesson taught the first school. It was a subscription school and was held in a small office building owned by Al Mathews and was located on the northeast corner of the lots now occupied by the city building. The school lasted from January to March 1885.

The first public school was held in a two-story building known as the Central Hotel and was located where the Fred Miller home is today. The first four grades were taught in this school. Miss Jennie Davey, deceased, of Anthony, was one of the teachers. The rest of the grades were taught in a building across the street south in an old building, where the Terrel Implement shed is now. Miss Lula Youngblood, who later was Mrs. Carrithers, was one of the teachers. Mrs. Carrithers, now deceased, was later County Superintendent. Also, Miss Davey, now deceased, was County Superintendent of Public Schools.

In January 1886, the school was moved to a new four-room brick building located at the north end of Main Street, where the present school now stands. It burned in 1916. Our present building was started in 1917, at the same location of the school built in 1886.

Roy Robinson was the first child born in Attica. Vern Day was the second, George F. Crowell was the third, and R. O. Williamson was the fourth.

There were plenty of drug stores, some of which sold drugs and some liquors. There were three Chinese laundries, three hotels and boarding houses, five lumberyards, nine doctors, five hardware stores, two furniture stores, seven grocery stores, five churches and numerous meat markets and barber shops and other business places. The population reached 3000.

Old-fashioned stage lines, drawn by from four to eight ponies or mules, were routed through Attica. Roads in those days were just trails without regard to section lines. The sidewalks were boardwalks, and hitching racks lined the streets. There were numerous livery barns which did a thriving business.

Attica was for some time the terminus of the railroad, and there were several acres of land used by the Santa Fe as storage for materials to be used in extending the railroad.

Swindlers and smooth-tongued men saw their chances for private gain, as was the case in most frontier towns. One project here was the bonding of the town for $36,900.00 with interest at 5 percent for the erection of a sugar mill and city water system. This sugar mill was built on the Ely farm of today, which is directly south of Attica and was located across the road west of the Homer Henderson farm home. The water stand-pipe, similar to the one still used in Harper, was near the sugar mill. The farmers grew cane for the sugar mill. The farmers, merchants and citizens were drawn into the project and their money used. For a time, everything looked rosy, then the whole thing blew up. The promoters shut down the mill and left town, owing individuals, businessmen and farmers, many of whom were left without money or livelihood. The little boom town was left with a useless sugar mill, a water system they could not afford to operate, and the town had the heavy debt, which seemed impossible to ever be paid off by people with so little money as most of the inhabitants had in those days. People were discouraged and for a time it seemed the town was doomed.

When the Cherokee Strip was opened, the town was almost depopulated, houses were vacated and sold for taxes, and most of the town was moved away. The people who were left were so discouraged that not a tree or shrub was planted. The real estate could not pay off the indebtedness, crop failure came year after year. People considered moving the town across the railroad tracks, out of the city limits, to escape payment of the bonds. In time, the debt was lessended to 33 1/3 percent with interest at 5 percent. Things took a turn for the better, and people were encouraged. The town began once again to improve and grow. This time there was no boom. The flour mill was built, the elevators came gradually and were the means of caring for the farmers and their crops. The farmers were educated in the production of crops suited to the vicinity.

Having paid off the fraudulent bonds, voted for a new water and sewage system, the city also planned for a municipal light and power system.

The original 24th Judicial District was established by Chapter 118, Laws of 1889, and consisted of Harper and Barber counties. In the election of Nov. 4, 1890, G. W. McKay of Attica was elected judge of the 24th District.

CHURCHES OF ATTICA
Assembly of God Church, Attica (1925)

The Attica Assembly of God was founded in 1925 by the Mehaney sisters, and was set in order by District Superintendent Fred Volger on November 28, 1926.

Before the church was built services were held at the home of Rev. Safford. The present church was erected under the pastorate of Rev. V. G. Greisen.

The Assembly supports two missionaries, Rev. Greisen, who served in Europe, and Rev. Stetz in Korea.

The membership as of this time is 34.

Faith Baptist Church, Attica

The Faith Baptist Church was incorporated October 11, 1946 with 14 members.

Services were held in the Brant Funeral Parlor until the church was built and dedicated February 19, 1950. The parsonage was purchased March 1, 1958.

The present membership is 80.

The Attica Christian Church (1912)

The Christian Church had its beginning in 1912 in the school building. A one-room building was the next venture and in 1915 the present structure was completed. In 1936 a gift of $1,000.00 from the estate of Mrs. Anna Menke enabled the congregation to re-roof and decorate the church.

The present membership is 150.

The Evangelical United Brethren Church, Attica (1885)

The Attica United Brethren Church was organized on Dec. 5, 1885, with 13 members.

The first building was destroyed by fire in 1902. Negotiations were made immediately for a new building, which was completed in 1903. By 1921 the congregation had grown to require a new building which was constructed and dedicated October 15, 1922. In November 1946, the United Brethren Church merged with the Evangelical Church.

On April 1, 1968, the Evangelical United Brethren Church merged with the Methodist organization. This church is now called the West Side United Methodist Church with a membership of 139.

The Attica Methodist Church (1886)

The Attica Methodist Church had its beginning on February 28, 1886 with an official board to carry on its work. The first building was a small frame structure. On cold winter mornings services were held in the local funeral parlor due to inadequate heating facilities.

The present brick structure was built in 1912-13. The present parsonage was purchased in 1918. The church celebrated its 75th anniversary in 1961. In April of 1968 this church became known as the Attica United Methodist Church.

The present membership is 284.

The Attica Southern Baptist Church (1956)

The First Southern Baptist Church is the most recently organzed church in Attica. Their first meeting was held in 1956. Pending a permanent home the group met in various public buildings. Belle Plaine was voted to be the mother church until the Attica group became self-supporting. The church building was completed in 1958. The present membership is 51.

Attica Index, June 24, 1936
GET $1,000 IN ATTICA BANK RAID

Armed Thugs Escape After Getting All Money in Sight; Miss Some

GIRL HOSTAGES UNHURT

Attica, Kan. June 24 (AP)—Armed bandits who held up the Attica State Bank and kidnapped two girl employees, later releasing them unharmed, obtained slightly less than $1,000 cash in a raid just before closing time today, cashier A. A. Hilliard estimated.

Four women, two employees and two customers, were in the bank when the bandits entered.

Forced to Lie on Floor

When Miss Maxine Hilliard, daughter of the cashier, and Miss Mildred Smith, also a bank employee, refused them admittance to the back room, the leader drew a pistol and commanded the four women to lie on the floor.

Another carrying a money bag ran behind the cages and scooped up all the money in sight. Some of the bank's cash was hidden.

Leaving Mrs. Wayman Craig and Mrs. Ralph Hoyt, the customers, in the bank, the bandits forced Miss Hilliard and Miss Smith to go with them.

A fourth man waited in the car.

Scatter Tacks

The two girls were released about two blocks from the bank. The robber scattered big tacks on the highway to hamper pursuit.

Hilliard said that the girls were treated "courteously" by the bandits, two of whom were described as dark complexioned and speaking broken English. All were described as "about thirty."

The gang escaped in a grey Ford, V-8, tudor sedan, going east on the highway. Hilliard said the car's license was 12, but that the others numbers were not obtained.

Heavily armed with shotguns and pistols, Sheriff Charley Hoover and two deputies, Al Bertrand and Ralph DeWitt, cruised the western part of the county during the afternoon and evening hoping to intercept the bandit car.

Bank Robbed Twice in 44 Years of Operation

Attica Index, date unknown

The First National Bank of Attica has been robbed twice in the nearly 44 years of operation, according to Mrs. Maxine McGuire, vice-president and cashier.

Chiseling out the back of the vault, robbers obtained a small amout of silver in a night robbery in 1917. The second robbery was staged in daylight on June 24, 1936. Mrs. McGuire and Mrs. Clarence Oliver remember the event quite vividly. They were taken by the robbers to the outskirts of town and released

Three men staged the robbery. One was killed in Enid, another was killed in Oklahoma City, and the third man is serving a life sentence in a federal penitentiary.

CRATER SPEWS GAS, WATER

Harper Advocate, Feb. 7, 1963

An innocent rumble that was noticed by a rabbit trapper early Thursday morning has developed into a phenomenon the likes of which this area and possibly the state has never seen.

George Colber, of Duquoin, was checking rabbit traps about six miles north of Attica when he heard a rumble like an explosion to the west of where he was. He investigated and saw the dirt spewing up in the air from a hole in the middle of the road six miles north and about three-fourths of a mile west of Attica. The hole was about seventeen feet in diameter at the time.

Now the "Old Faithful" has a crater nearly 50 feet across.

First to come out of the crater was gas and dirt, then gas and mud created by the mixture of fresh water and dirt. On Friday the water began changing to salt water and the mud thinned out.

John Roberts, assistant director of the conservation division of the State Corporation Commission, was immediately notified and the investigation was started.

At first it was thought that the gas might be surface gas or stray shallow gas that was released because of the thawing of the ground that had been frozen two or three feet deep.

This theory was discarded when the eruption continued to belch gas, mud and water with almost the same pressure it had soon after it started. This, along with the fact that the water was from fresh to salt, indicated that it was coming from a greater depth.

Checking the area around the crater revealed many other smaller eruptions in the Antrim pasture south of the large crater. These ranged in size from a few inches to about 12 or 15 feet in diameter. Bill Carr, farmer living south of the crater, counted 28 smaller holes in the mile south of the big hole.

By Friday night the activity in the smaller holes had subsided and only a few bubbles indicated they had been working.

Meanwhile, oil operators in the immediate area of the eruptions were working together to determine the source of the gas. Roberts said it was natural gas because it had been tested and that it burns, but there was little danger as gas dissipates quickly into the air.

Salt Water Problem

The salt water that is being tossed out of the hole and into Bluff Creek is posing a problem for farmers who have cattle in fields along the creek.

In tests taken Monday, a concentration of 10,000 parts of chloride to a million parts of water was indicated at the lip of the crater. One and two miles below the crater, the concentration was 25,000 and 23,000 parts per million, respectively, while at the U.S. 160 bridge east of Attica, the count was 2,500. It even showed up in the creek west of Anthony with a count of 880 parts per million.

Some of the farmers who have had to move stock, string fences, or otherwise make arrangements to prevent the cattle from drinking too much salt water, are Bill Carr, Marion Arb, Fred Brown, Grant Martin and Dan Stewart.

Oil men were meeting Wednesday with representatives of the Corporation Commission at Wichita to work out a plan of attack on the geyser.

The oil men were called together by John Roberts of the commission. "Ten or fifteen producers in the immediate 1½ mile area around the hole will organize this thing," he said.

There are about 40 oil and gas wells producing and plugged in the 1½ mile circle. The whole Spivey-Grabb field has 400 to 500 wells.

All the wells are suspects. Roberts reasoned that it was unlikely the sudden volcano had a base 4,400 feet down in the Mississippian strata formation that provided the oil and gas for the Spivey-Gragg field.

"It's likely that the gas and oil channeled up in, or around a well," he said. "Then it met a soft strata and rose gradually with it to ground level."

Roberts said, however, that a breach in either a producing or plugged well or a pipeline could be causing the geyser.

"Pressure on the spurting hole has died down some since last weekend," Roberts said. Peak of the pitching mineral and mud is about 15 feet. Conservation men, aided by oil field workers, have been moving from well to well in a widening circle around the hole. On the producing wells, they check the pressure to see if any gas is being lost. On the plugged wells, they dig down to where the pipe has been sealed off, four feet of frozen ground, check the well with a stethoscope to listen for the rush of gas and water.

Oil men are concerned because the geyser is the responsibility of the company that drilled the hole that is the source. Roberts said he would hesitate to block off the geyser for fear of forcing salt water into the town wells of Attica, six miles to the southeast.

Meanwhile the vanishing natural gas is causing little damage to the field. According to Roberts, the geyser is not making as much gas as a good gas well will, even under pro-ration.

THE FIRST NATIONAL BANK OF ATTICA

This bank was opened for business March 19, 1913, with a capital stock of $25,000. The first officers were V. B. Ballard, President; R. O. Williamson, Vice-President; A. M. McBride, Cashier; A. A. Hilliard, Assistant Cashier. The directors were Ballard, Williamson, McBride, W. A. Miller and Stanley Shuk.

W. A. Miller was sent to Washington, D.C., to secure the charter.

The bank building was completely remodeled in 1955.

In 1941, A. A. Hilliard became president and served in this capacity until his death in 1953.

This bank celebrated its 50th anniversary in 1953.

This organization is still operated by members of the Hilliard family.

The following is an inscription on a tombstone in the Attica, Kansas, cemetery: "Through this inscription I wish to enter my dying protest against what is called the Democratic Party. I have watched it closely since the days of Jackson and I know all the misfortunes of our nation, have come through the so-called party. Therefore beware of this party of treason. Put on in fulfillment of promise to the deceased."

N. Grigsby died April 16, 1890, aged 78 years, 6 months and 5 days. 2nd Lt., Co. G., 10th Ind. Cavalry.

(This man married Lincoln's oldest sister.)

Turtle Races in Attica

Every town has its people that are willing to give of themselves that others may have pleasure and enjoyment. Attica is no exception.

Selma Kernohan was a lover of children so she conceived the idea of having turtle races. Selma furnished the turtles for the first race, giving prizes to the winners and candy and cakes to all who came.

The first races were by invitation; however, in 1960 the races were open to all children. Later they were expanded to include mothers and grandmothers.

The project became an annual affair and approximately two hundred children were present in 1962. In 1965 the 20 and 4 club became the sponsors as the project was too large for Selma and her helpers to handle.

Mrs. Kernohan was always present to make the awards. 1967 was her last race, she passed away in February 1968, a living memory to thousands of children.

Present Day Attica —
The City of Beautiful Flowers

Attica now has a population of 822.

In 1968 the State Senate and House of Representatives enacted legislation allowing Attica to become a unified district (school). The enrollment of the Attica schools, before unification, stands at 273 students. The school libraries contain 3,389 books.

There are 3,148 volumes in the public library.

The post office is located on Main Street and the building was erected in 1961.

Attica has two lodges, Masonic and O.E.S. There are two civic organizations, Lions Club and Civic Club.

The Attica newspaper is a weekly publication called the *Attica Independent* and its editor is B. E. Jacobsen.

Attica Hospital District has much of the following equipment: Cardiac Monitor, Bird Respirator, Defibulator, Heart Pacer, EKG machine, heated bassinet in delivery room, oxygen piped to rooms and emergency rooms, nursery equipped with incubator, and fully equipped laboratory and X-ray equipment.

Dr. W. P. Niles is Chief-of-Staff.

Bluff Creek

Little is known of the forming of Bluff Creek. Its location is as follows: northwest one-fourth of section 24, township 34, range 5 west. The first postmaster was G. S. Reid and the post office opened July 24, 1878, and was moved to Bluff in February 1887.

From *The Anthony Republican,* Jan. 23, 1879

Bluff Creek is five and three-fourths miles north of the state line and three-fourths miles west of Sumner-Harper county line. It is the residence of S. G. Reid, the postmaster. It was established July 24, 1878 in answer to the prayers of the thirty-eight petitioners. It is a special office supplied with mail from Caldwell. We hope to have a mail route from Caldwell via Doster, Sumner County and this place to Anthony.

Bluff

We can not be absolutely sure of the location of the Bluff post office. The postal department records its establishment as being February 1, 1887 with Robert Echols as the first postmaster. Bluff was closed January 28, to reopen as Bluff City post office. Whether the location of "Bluff" and "Bluff City" is the same, we can not be sure, but we assume that Bluff was near the present Bluff City.

Bluff City

JAMES GLOVER PITCHED TENT AT
BLUFF CITY 75 YEARS AGO

By Alberta Brittain Cook

From "The Caldwell Messenger," July 10, 1961

On Oct. 6, 1886 the late James Glover pitched his tent on the present site of Bluff City. He came from Arkansas City in the interest of the Border Line Town and Land Company of which James N. Young of Chicago was president and Edward P. Green was secretary.

The representatives of the Land Company were working in the interest of building and construction of the St. Louis, Kan. and Southwestern Railroad which merged on Jan. 1, 1887 with the Great St. Louis and San Francisco System. The first depot that was built was one of the finest on the line west of St. Louis.

Bluff City was platted November 20, 1886 and the first lots were sold on that day. Four weeks later, $35,000 worth of lots had been sold and about 200 men had moved in with their families and were busily engaged in the construction of about 40 buildings for the new town. All building materials were hauled 16 miles by wagon from Caldwell.

The first newspaper, *The Tribune,* was printed in an incompleted building on December 30, 1886 with Will C. Barnes as the editor. *The Tribune* was followed by the *Herald, The Independent, The Messenger* and the *News* which was published by Mrs. Ed Strunk for more than a quarter of a century when it was sold to the Anthony *Republican* on Dec. 30, 1956.

The Border Line Town and Land Company has erected a thirty-room hotel complete in all its apportionments.

All this was done in the space of four weeks.

The improvements which the railroad company will put at Bluff City are to be of the most substantial and complete character. The plans for the roundhouse, freight house and car repair shops are now complete. The part of the road from Beaumont to Bluff City, 107 miles, will be known as the Bluff City division and will be operated from this point.

Eleven acres were set aside for a park which was first named Walnut Grove, but was later changed to Glover Park in honor of the late James Glover, who did the landscaping and most of the planting of the trees and shrubs and could rightfully be called the "Father" of our town. The park became quite famous for its beauty and was classed as one of the most beautiful parks in the United States. The late Charles M. Loring, eminent authority on parks, once stated that it was the most beautiful and the largest per capita park in the world.

The music talent of this section has always been above average and between 1896 and 1910 Bluff City boasted a splendid band. Every other Sunday a band concert was held in the park with people driving many miles to attend.

In the religious work in the early days, the Christian, Methodist and Catholic churches were quite active.

At the time of the founding of Bluff City a one-room schoolhouse was erected one half mile south of town. It was later replaced by a four-room, two story brick building which was located only a few feet west of the present structure. For a number of years the original brick structure was used for both grade school and a two year high school. While our grade school has always been above average, a need for higher education was apparent at an early period in the history of the town. About seventy years ago, James Glover, the first settler, noticed that some of our best citizens moved away in order to give their children the benefit of higher learning. They seldom came back, and the thought came to him, "Why not a township high school?"

In the fall of 1890, Mr. Glover corresponded with our state representative, George Coulson, who had been elected on the Alliance Ticket. He thought well of the plan and presented the bill to his Alliance constituents for their approval. This bill was passed and may be found in Sessions Laws of 1903, Page 691, Chapter 452, Page 693, Chapter 453. The bill authorized Stohrville Township to establish and maintain a high school. Two years later we had our Representative W. M. Moore introduce a bill making it statewide and it was approved. Bluff Citians have always been proud that one of its own citizens conceived and enacted the law under which our splendid high school was established in 1925.

The founders of Bluff City had dreams of a population of 10,000 and did boast of almost 1,000 at one time, but when the railroad shops and roundhouse were moved to Anthony it caused a large portion of our population to move. Several families moved when the Cherokee Strip was opened to settlement in 1893, but the moving of the railroad shops caused the greatest loss.

A large portion of the business section of the town was destroyed by fire as most of the original buildings were frame structures.

The bank building, one of the original structures, has stood as a landmark through the years; however, the banking facilities were moved to the Citizens National Bank in Anthony in the late 1930's.

Bluff City has been governed by a Mayor and a five member Council.

Notes taken from the obituary of James Glover published in the *Bluff City News,* 1924.

Born in White Sands, Prince Edward Island, August 22, 1839, died March 17, 1924.

As a young man he moved to New York State where he worked in the textile mills.

Later he moved to Ohio and engaged in the mercantile business. He enlisted in 110 Ohio Volunteers. He was mustered out of the service in 1869 at Mason, Iowa.

In 1885 he came to Udall, Kansas.

In October 1886, he came to Bluff City and pitched his tent in a cornfield.

Became a director of the K.S.W. Railroad.

Donated land for city park. Planted most of the trees and shrubs in the park.

He landscaped the courthouse grounds in Anthony.

Mayor of Bluff City for sixteen years.

He was author of the Kansas Township High School Law.

Postmaster for many years.

Director of the State Bank of Bluff City. Was vice-president at the time of his death.

In 1887 he married Sarah J. Moody. Their children are Fred S. Glover, Anthony, Kansas; Kenneth M. Glover, Kansas City and Mrs. T. L. Sturdevant.

Pioneer Doctors in the Bluff City Area

Dr. Bundie Neil operated the first drug store in Bluff City. Other doctors were Dr. Frisk, Dr. Arnold, Dr. Bowls and Dr. Cutler W. Goodrich.

Bluff City Deer Farm

Joseph H. Lewis pre-empted 160 acres of land from the United States government as soon as the county was organized. He added to this farm from time to time until he owned 400 acres.

His deer park contained about 30 acres densely shaded by

catalpas, maples, black walnut and apple trees. The park was enclosed with an eight foot steel woven wire fence. The herd of 100 deer originated from only one pair and were the delightful pets of "Uncle Joe."

The woods were full of deer, red squirrels and turkeys. Kentucky thoroughbreds and fine cattle were to be found in his pastures.

(United) Bluff City Methodist Church (1891)

The Methodist Church was organized in 1891 by Rev. Charles Brown. The church was made a part of the Freeport charge until the Bluff City was organized with Burchfiel and Grandview (both schoolhouses).

Services were held in the old Hybsha Hall until the new church building was completed.

In 1892 the Burchfiel and Grandview appointments were added to the town. This made up the "Bluff City Charge." A few years later Grandview was dropped and Cameron was added.

The building was destroyed by fire November 14, 1914. It was rebuilt and dedicated December 24, 1916.

The present membership of the church is 76.

Christian Church, Bluff City

Members of this early church held their meetings in Pleasant Hill and Arnold schoolhouses. Later a building 24 x 30 feet was moved from Rome to serve the congregation. On July 5, 1893, a charter was granted to the congregation. The present church building was built in 1939. The cherished bell from the early church still summons all to worship.

The present membership of the church is 40.

PRESENT DAY BLUFF CITY

The population of Bluff City is 135. There is an elementary school with 49 students and six teachers. The post office is located on Main Street, the building was constructed in 1886. There is one rural route operating from this post office. The Mason, O.E.S. and Rebekah lodges are active in Bluff City. There are two churches in Bluff City, the Methodist with 79 members, and the Christian with 40 members.

Cameron-Camchester

The date of earliest nucleus of the village of Cameron eludes us but a trading post probably came into being in the late '80's. The first authentic record that we have of the town is the establishment of the post office on June 2, 1893 with Milton S. Foster as postmaster.

Before the coming of the railroad (Hutchinson and Southern, later called the Missouri Pacific), mail was brought in by hack from Anthony and Harper.

Sometime in the history of the town there was supposed to have been a population of 300 with a saloon, gambling house, lumberyard, a drugstore operated by Dr. Lucas, three grocery stores and a blacksmith shop.

Cameron became a cattle shipping center with the coming of the railroads. In the 1902 atlas the city map of Cameron shows it as having been laid out in a 31 block area, in Spring Township. Its location was the southwest one-fourth of section 13, township 35 south, range 7 west.

The Atchison, Topeka, and Santa Fe Railroad came in about 1902.

Cameron had the reputation of being a wild, rough town due to the fact that it bordered the "Outlet" and was a mecca for cowboys.

From "Pioneer Story," by L. N. Lydick

"In 1893 the announcement was made by the government that the 'Cherokee Strip' would be thrown open for settlement on Sept. 16, and that the little town of Cameron was made a place for registration. Within a few days Cameron's population increased from a few dozen inhabitants to 10,000. Men stood in line for days in order not to lose their turn to register for a chance to make a race for a free farm. Standing room in the long line was at a high premium. Various schemes were inaugurated in an effort to get into the booth, but so strict were the watchers that such attempts usually failed. A resourceful middle-aged lady, however, originated a unique plan that worked. Walking hurriedly to the door of the registration building, bare headed and wearing a white kitchen apron, she carried a tray containing several cups of hot coffee. She was immediately given the right of way, and when once inside the building her coffee became of secondary importance, and she received her registration certificate without delay.

It was at this time that Manchester, Oklahoma, was born. Manchester was a competitor to Cameron, Kansas, just across the state line. The contest between the two towns was bitter in the extreme. In order to take a middle attitude the railway depot was oved to a location half-way between the two towns and its name changed to "Camchester," a combination of the two names, Cameron and Manchester. Cameron, composed of aggressive men was not to be so easily outwitted and Cameron's name was officially changed to "Camchester" to correspond with the railroad station. The post office name was automatically changed to Camchester. Thus Camchester had both the post office and the railroad in name even if it did not have the actual physical possession of the depot, which was on the Oklahoma side. As the long town fight continued several of the Camchester business houses and dwellings were burned, presumably from incendiary origin. However, as time passed, one by one the remaining Camchester buildings were moved across the state line and the fight was eventually over, much to the comfort of all concerned, including the aggressive editor of the community paper the "Manchester Journal."

The Cameron post office was discontinued February 2, 1900. Camchester was established February 2, 1900 with Thos. B. Smith as postmaster. The Camchester post office closed March 31, 1903.

Cora City

Cora City is best described by the following clipping from the Anthony *Journal,* October 24, 1878: "Cora City was laid out and located April 16, 1877. The gender of the infant, not suiting all parties, underwent a metamorphosis and now answers to the name of Harper City. It is located six and one-half miles from the north of the county."

Corwin

As researched by A. L. Griesinger

The town of Corwin was named for Oscar A. Corwin who owned the west one-half of section 20, township 34, range 9 west. His residence was at the extreme northwest corner. He operated a general store from this location. On August 20, 1883 Mr. Corwin was appointed postmaster. Jess Scantlin, driving a mule to a cart, carried the mail from Corwin to Hazelton. Mr. Scantlin later married Mr. Corwin's daughter.

In 1886, when the railroad was built one and one-half miles from old Corwin, a new Corwin was started at the present site. Mr. Hittle settled at the new Corwin where he built a residence and a store. Mr. Hittle bought prairie chickens from the early settlers for twenty cents each and shipped them to Kansas City and St. Louis.

Jim F. Andrews built a hotel and was the second postmaster. At one time Corwin boasted a race track. The track was built by G. R. Landers at the southwest corner of town.

Dutch Andrews, grandson of J. F. Andrews, gave the following account: "G. R. Landers became a big cattle man and many farmers in the area sold corn to him for 10 cents per bushel. In the blizzard of 1903 all of Lander's cattle froze to death. Facing financial ruin, he boarded a train and was never heard from again. J. F. Andrews and others skinned the cattle and sold their hides for $2.50 apiece."

From the 'Kansas cyclopedia' 1912 publication we quote: "Corwin, a village in Blaine township, is a station on the Missouri Pacific Railroad, 17 miles southwest of Anthony, county seat. It has a money order post office, telegraph and express office, telephone connections, hotel, a good local trade and in 1910 reported a population of 125. At one time Corwin had two grocery stores, two blacksmith shops, two hotels, one elevator, two restaurants, two livery barns, a church, a bank, a lumberyard, a two-story school building which included two years of high school and a winning baseball team."

At the present time Corwin has about 20 citizens, a modern Farmer Coop Elevator and office, an old-fashioned grocery store that has been operated by Helen Dennis for the past forty years. There is no church or school.

Crisfield

Crisfield, a town located in western Harper County; the legal description is: southeast one-fourth, section 17, township 33, south, range 9 west. The town had its beginning in 1883, a year before the Southern Kansas Railroad was extended from Attica.

The area post office was located north of Crisfield at Otego. In February 1885 the Otego post office was moved to Crisfield with William H. Ranke as postmaster, this office was closed in 1951.

At one time Crisfield was considered a boom town with an estimated population of 1,500. The Atlas of 1886 shows the town plat to be laid out in a twenty-two block area, with an unplatted portion owned by the Camp Town Company. Early business establishments were: two hotels, two banks, four livery stables, four grocery stores, a grain elevator, two lumberyards, and a drugstore. A newspaper, the *Crisfield Courier,* was established in 1885, Charles Wilson, editor. This enterprise was discontinued in 1889. There was a school and a Methodist church located in the town.

Crisfield probably owes its short life to the lack of a sufficient water supply. No living water was nearby and good wells could not be procured. Serious fires continuously plagued the community.

The Atchison, Topeka, and Santa Fe assumed control of the original Southern Kansas Railroad.

In 1886 the post office was located on the corner of Main Street and Sixth Avenue. The church was in the north one-half of block 15 on Seventh Avenue, and the hotel on east Main Street.

Dr. Cleveland was one of the pioneer doctors. Dental work was also performed by the family physician, usually a chair was placed outside of the house and the tooth extracted. The patient was allowed a chew of tobacco (probably to keep down infection).

Mr. and Mrs. L. N. Hughbanks, now living in Hutchinson, are one of the pioneer families of the Crisfield area. Mrs. Hughbanks was a newspaper correspondent for the Anthony *Republican.*

Jim Russel Crow, store owner and rock mason, along with Phil Payne started the Payne and Crow Animal Company in

1889. Jackrabbits were caught for coursing meets and were shipped to Wichita where they were sent on to New York and England. Some time later Ira, Jude and John Crow joined the company. Four spools of netting, 3,000 feet each in length and four feet high were used to capture the rabbits.

From *The Attica Independent*, February 1911

Crisfield is booming, F. F. McMullin has a new blacksmith shop, his son, Jack, runs the dry goods and grocery store and they recently bought the hardware store. A. S. Vance has a good lumberyard and grain business. H. J. Mandeville has the hotel.

Mrs. Russelle Hollister Shaw, now of Canadian, Texas, attended the Crisfield and Diamond Valley schools and taught the Diamond Valley School from 1940 to 1946.

In 1918 the population was 47. A cyclone severely damaged the town in 1923.

Mr. and Mrs. Lonnie Reneau were the last residents of Crisfield. Mrs. Reneau was the postmaster when the post office was discontinued.

The Crisfield Methodist Church (Disbanded)

The Crisfield Methodist church was organized around 1900 and the church building was erected in 1910. The congregation thrived and served the surrounding community for many years. Due to the declining population services were discontinued in 1940; however, Sunday school was held there for some time.

All that remains of Crisfield is the memory and the sign on the Atchison, Topeka, and Santa Fe Railroad.

Crystal Springs

From the "Kansas Cyclopedia," 1912

Crystal Springs, a little village in Lake Township, Harper County, is a station on the Atchison, Topeka, & Santa Fe Railroad about half-way between Harper and Attica. It has a post office, an express office, telephone connections, and in 1910 reported a population of 38.

The Crisfield post office was established January 16, 1885, with Mrs. Naomi L. Bukins as postmaster.

Crystal Springs Church (disbanded)

The Methodist Church at Crystal Springs was dedicated just before the cyclone of 1892, when it was partially destroyed. The building was repaired and the Crystal Springs congregation helped to organize the Silver Creek Church. Most of their ministers were circuit preachers from Harper and Attica. The building was sold to the Silver Creek Church in 1910.

PRESENT DAY CRYSTAL SPRINGS

The present population is 25. Crystal Springs is in the Attica unified school district. The post office is located in the residence of the postmaster, Miss Miller.

The present-day business establishments are: one grocery store, a slaughter and meat processing plant with locker service, enjoys an especially fine reputation, a service station and bulk oil plant, a machine shop and a grain elevator.

The legal description of Crystal Springs is northeast one-fourth, section 13, township 32, south, range 8 west.

When the Amish Mennonite settlers arrived in Harper County, Crystal Springs consisted of a depot, a post office, a blacksmith shop, stockyards and two grain elevators; in addition there were four dwelling houses. Probable date 1890.

Curran

The Curran post office was located in the southwest one-fourth of section 23 (township) 31 south, range 8 west, on land owned by J. C. Curran. The post office was opened April 27, 1892 and was discontinued November 30, 1903. According to the Harper County Atlas of 1902 Curran was the only post office in Garden Township.

Duquoin

On May 10, 1882, Chester A. Arthur, President of the United States, signed documents giving William O. Butler ownership of the south one-half of the northwest one-fourth, section 3, township 31, range 7 west. Recorded in Book E, page

83. It was on this location that the village of Duquoin was built. The post office was opened May 23, 1893 with Walter E. Fitch as postmaster. In 1910 there was a telegraph and express office, general stores, two grain elevators and a flour mill. The population was 75.

At the present time the population is 13. One two-teacher school with 20 students is located three miles south of Duquoin. The post office is located at Pine and Main and was built in 1912. Duquoin now has an elevator with 200,000 bushel capacity, a grocery store and the Church of Christ with 35 members.

Three of the original town promoters were Dave Brown, Newt Brown and Thomas Craig.

Legend has it that the first Duquoin was located one mile south and one mile west of the present location. We found no records to this effect; however, this is probably the case and the post office was moved to the new townsite on the railroad and the new town carried the name of the already established post office.

Embry

The town of Embry was located five miles east and one mile north of Anthony. The legal description is northeast one-fourth of section 23, and northwest one-fourth of section 24, township 33 south, range 6 west. The town was laid out in sixteen blocks being four blocks long and four blocks wide. Main Street extended north and south dividing the town equally. The town was located on the St. Louis, Fort Scott and Wichita Railroad. The post office was established Dec. 15, 1885 and was discontinued November 5, 1889. The first postmaster was William F. Stocker. Nothing remains of the town today.

Freeport and Midlothian

By Grace Ransom and Josephine Greve

Few people outside of those living in the Freeport community know that Freeport was once two towns, Freeport and Midlothian.

In 1878 there was a small trading post and post office operated by B. H. Freeman, located two or three miles southeast of
the present site of Freeport. The mail was brought twice a week
by stage from Gourock. The stage line extended from Wellington to Medicine Lodge. The Midlothian post office was established April 19, 1878.

In 1885, the St. Louis, Fort Scott, and Wichita Railroad
built a line to Anthony. With the advent of the railroad, Mr.
Freeman moved his post office to the Midlothian-Freeport area.

On February 27, 1885, the Freeport town plot was filed for
record. It consisted of 46 acres of Joseph Haun's farm; located
on southwest one-fourth of section 3, township 33 south, range
5 west. On June 1, T. B. Marsh, one of the oldest residents of
Harper County, assumed the management of the town company.

The town of Midlothian received its charter eight days after
that of Freeport. The tract of 48 acres was purchased from Herg-
et and Blakely, the legal description being: southeast one-fourth
of section 4, township 33 south, range 5 west and the northeast
one-fourth section 9, township 33 south, range 5 west.

Immediately following the town's organization, each town
started its own newspaper. The Freeport newspaper was known
as the *Freeport Leader,* the Midlothian as the *Midlothian Sun.*
After being published for six months the *Sun* was moved to
Freeport and its name changed to the *Freeport Tribune.*

The two towns lay practically side by side, they were joined
by Grand Avenue which extended north and south.

Human nature being what it is there developed a difference
of opinion in some areas, one being the placement of the depot,
which was eventually built at the east end of Freeport's Main
Street.

Bitter feelings developed and the towns became hostile toward
each other until, traditions say, they went so far as to build
a fence down the middle of Grand Avenue. Tempers flared, but
according to the *Freeport Tribune,* dated March 18, 1886, their
differences had been settled and Midlothian became known as
West Freeport.

Midlothian took its name from a Scotch word meaning 'mid-
land.'

After the friendly settlement of their differences, Freeport
grew and prospered and in 1886, the following business places
are recorded: two grain elevators, three lumberyards, three

coal yards, two newspapers, two hotels, one bank, five dry goods stores, nine grocery stores, three drug stores, two implement houses, two hardware stores, two meat markets, four blacksmith shops, one harness shop, one millinery store, one billiard hall, two land and loan offices, three grain buyers and two barber shops.

From 1885 to 1893 Freeport had its greatest growth. In 1887 there were 300 residents and by 1892 the number had increased to 700. Many of these people had moved to Freeport to await the opening of the Cherokee Outlet which took place, September 16, 1893, and overnight Freeport nearly became a ghost town. The 1895 census shows Freeport as having only 54 inhabitants. By 1910 the population was 161.

Mr. Schmidt was one of the town's leading citizens, having founded the Freeport State Bank which is still in operation. He served in many civic capacities.

The town of Freeport became an incorporated city of the third class on October 12, 1887 and today is known as the smallest incorporated city in Kansas. The town is governed by a Mayor and council but has had no elections in the past decade. W. H. Pohlenz was mayor for twenty years, and he said, "Elections cost money, so we stopped having them." Ben Brooks is the present mayor of Freeport, elected by the voters of Silver Creek Township.

The first schoolhouse was in the old town of Freeport and was a two-story wood structure which was destroyed by fire in 1908. It was replaced by a concrete structure which was designed without enough windows. The school was immediately dubbed "The jail." This building was replaced by a three-room brick structure. The Freeport school is now a part of a unified district.

There have been two churches identified with Freeport. The Methodist, after various meeting places obtained a church building in 1896 and was used until it was destroyed by fire in 1930. The Presbyterian Church was organized in 1884 and is still active in the community.

The Tay Zay Voo Study and Social Club, organized in 1921, purchased the Freeport Cemetery from the Pohl Estate for $200. After a general improvement and beautification plan, they obtained a state charter and in turn presented it to the town of Freeport. In 1926, they succeeded in organizing the Freeport Cemetery Association.

The Freeport Library Association was organized in 1926. A building was purchased on Main Street and a public library was maintained for many years. Due to lack of interest the library was recently closed and the property sold.

Freeport once boasted a police force but no one seems to recall there ever having been a jail in town. There is still a fire department, although the machinery is of ancient vintage and needs a volunteer fire fighting crew to pull it from place to place and pump it by hand. The town estimates that the machinery will soon be museum pieces.

In the 82 years of Freeport's existence there have been extensive losses by fire: a lumberyard, five cafes, a general store, a recreation parlor, a newspaper office, a hotel, a bank, two schoolhouses and a church.

The Freeport Elevator Company is in its 67th year of business and the Freeport State Bank is now in its 65th year of banking, with Leo Drouhard, President and Ben Brooks, Cashier.

At the present time the population of Freeport is 30, the grade school is in unified district No. 361 with an enrollment of 29. This is a two-teacher school. The school library has 800 volumes. The post office is located one-half block west of the cross-road. There is one R.F.D. route out of this office.

Lodges: O.E.S. No. 446, Masons No. 389, and R.N.A.

Freeport supports a strong 4-H club, The Freeport Trailblazers.

The Freeport Presbyterian Church (1884)

The church was organized in February, 1885, with 14 charter members. The church charter was granted March 17, 1886.

A church building was erected on the present site and the first services were held in April 1886. This church was organized as a home mission church but has been self-supporting since 1904. The present membership is 122.

THE FREEPORT STATE BANK

A charter was issued to the Freeport State Bank January 7, 1902. The organizing directors were P. G. Walton, C. A. Schmidt, Sam L. Smith, C. A. Gwinn and Sophia Schmidt. The capital stock was $5,000.00, on March 24, 1905; the stock was increased to $10,000.00, on June 16, 1959.

The following people have served as president of the Freeport

Bank: P. G. Walton, February 28, 1902; Sam L. Smith, March 11, 1911; A. J. Hilliard, January 1, 1919; C. A. Schmidt, June 3, 1926; Anna S. McGovney, July 1, 1948; W. F. Easter, June 1, 1959 and Leo F. Drouhard, July 26, 1961.

Statement of condition of the Freeport State Bank at the close of business December 31, 1967, shows the total assets to be $854,992.62.

The present officers are Leo F. Drouhard, President; Henry E. Schmidt, Vice-Pres.; Herbert N. Schmidt, Vice-Pres.; Ben Brooks, Cashier; Henry E. Stehle, Secretary of Board and Leafy E. Brooks, Asst. Cashier.

From a Diary of THEO. B. MARSH

Compiled by Kathryn L. Bottoroff

Harper County, Kansas, became a matter of history dating from the spring of 1878 at which time the county was organized, extending the early settlements of the great state westward towards the setting sun.

On July 5, 1878, Wichita, then a small frontier town on the banks of the Arkansas River and the terminus of a Santa Fe branch south from Newton, was the closest railroad to Harper County, from there it was necessary to take the stagecoach, hitched to four bronchos which stopped in Wellington and Caldwell.

Edward M. Moss and family and twelve other young families all from Peoria County, Illinois, near Jubilee, formed an early colony in the settlement of Silver Creek Valley on the Eastern border of Harper County, just over the line of Sumner County in response to the call of Uncle Sam to settle and build up a new part of his great domain, they had journeyed hither, driven their stakes and filed their claims adjoining each other on this beautiful tract of Indian Osage Trust land.

Harper, Kansas, about this time was boasting of a public inn called the Glenn House, a few other cabins and a lot of tents.

The beginning of Anthony was a few shacks, a lot of tents and a limited stock of provisions for sale from the rear end of an immigrant. wagon. Isaac Forbes, A. R. Blackburn, A. M. Lee and O. Jennings were some of the leading men in this town and O. Jennings was the first Mayor of Anthony.

By autumn the Santa Fe R.R. had extended its line to Wellington.

In the spring of 1879 a school was needed for the children, so we (Theo. B. Marsh) gave up a front room for a school room, and Miss Mary Jordan was the teacher. On Sunday this room was used for church services; this Colony were all members of the Protestant Episcopal faith. Name of Church with Cemetery was Trinity.

In the spring of 1880 this Colony erected a small school on the NW corner of 11-33-5, which was afterwards known as District No. 42, the cost of which was met by subscription, and Miss Mary Jordan continued to teach this school for many years. The same year our church people erected a little church, with a recess chancel in the east, at the cost of $1,000.00, including the seats, chancel, furniture and organ, each family paying their proper share of the cost, and Mr. Benjamin Freeman, the eldest member of the colony deeded three acres from the South end of his Claim to the Diocese of Kansas, for Church and Cemetery purposes, and as the Priest could only be there for one service a month, Freeman was appointed by the Bishop Vail as a layman, thus Church Services every Sunday. The shrubs to beautify the grounds were mailed here from Sherrill Chamberlain, Jubilee, Illinois.

Mr. Freeman also devoted the front room of his little house to the use of a post office and store for the convenience of the colony, which was known as Midlothian. The mail sack was carried twice a week from Gourock (afterwards became a R.R. station called Albion) 5½ miles N on the banks of the Chikaskia River, situated on the stage line from Wellington to Medicine Lodge.

The stock of groceries was replenished from time to time from Wellington, 28 mi. due east, then the terminus of the Santa Fe branch from Newton—which road graded a track and laid the rails a mile and one-half north of Midlothian as far as Silver Creek, en route from Anthony—this was in 1881 when one Sunday of that year we were astonished to behold a great number of men with a long train of flat cars, begin to take up this track and load these cars with ties and rails for a distance of over 30 miles to the east, then the following spring make a new survey straight west from Wellington to Harper, much to the chagrin of Anthony, the established County Seat, but four years later in 1885 the Missouri Pacific system was built from Wichita to Anthony and located a station called Freeport, 1 mile north and 2 miles west of Midlothian P.O. and store, which the following year were moved to this R.R. Station.

In these years of 1880 to 1883, our laws compelled all settlers to make proof of their claims, take their papers to the Wichita land office with $200.00 and receive the final receipt for which later a U.S. Patent would be issued to each settler, the towns being quite far from our settlement, our people knowing that I had acquired a business education desired that I should apply to our Governor for a Notarial Commission and Seal, which could save them and their witnesses many long weary miles of travel. Oh, then you may know that our little home became the center of much bustle and activity for many long months, as settlers came from near and far, each to wait their turn with two witnesses, for their final proofs to be properly executed and sealed, our premises became one great camp for days and days as they came and went.

Coal was high and far away, and wood was hauled 35 miles from the forks of Pond and Osage Creek in the Indian Territory, which took four days.

Corn, potatoes, pumpkins and turnips rewarded constant toil in the field. (The corn was shelled by small hand shellers requiring a hard long day's work to shell one load) which paid 75 cents per bushel, same for turnips.

By the spring of 1880 26 new settlers were in this area.

As cutting wood was considered a trespass, they were often stopped by the Mounted Police and compelled to unload. When police were out of sight, they returned for the wood.

The first sheep in this area were purchased near Augusta in Butler County, at $5.00 each, but fences always being poor, sheep were sold and cattle and hogs bought. The last clipping of the soft wool was exchanged for warm blankets at woolen mills of Blue Rapids. The few cows were good milkers, and besides supplying the family 17 lbs. were sent to Anthony, but money was scarce, and it was exchanged for one-half bushel of Osage Orange Hedge seed, planted in rows 3 ft. apart—set out hedge rows all around the Claim also surrounded the SW 40 and the orchard and garden, beside selling forty thousand plants to neighbors at three dollars per thousand. So $120.00, own fences for 17 lbs. of butter, plus work.

By 1885 the railroad had pushed its way on to Freeport and thence on to Anthony. In the meantime, the towns and county rapidly grew to greater proportions. Before Freeport was laid out at the SW corner of 3-33-5 then a townsite was located adjoining on Sect. 4 and named Mid Lothian, after our post office. The town company, being made up of farmers, of whom Simeon Singer was a leading spirit. Mr. Freeman, the store keeper and postmaster, was induced to join the company and obtained the government's consent to move the post office to this new town; then the railroad townsite put up a lively fight for its existence; for merchants, grain elevator men located their stores and elevators on this site, beside the depot and real estate office and a good hotel erected by the Freeport Town Co., with myself (Theo B. Marsh) duly appointed as Agent, and the Company finally had the P.O. name changed to Freeport to correspond with the name of the R.R. station.

A good boom was spreading over the towns of Kansas in the years 1885 and 1886, and Anthony being the terminus of the Mo. Pac. R.R. after the same pushed on from Freeport, was then the Center of a Red Hot Boom. Prices of lots in Anthony reached fabulous sums; large buildings sprang into existence.

McDowell and Hutchinson, were the publishers of the *Anthony Bulletin*.

Dr. Callender was the dentist.

Hubbard Livery Barn was on Jennings Avenue.

Dr. Bowers was practicing here in 1887.

On April 19, 1892, Uncle Sam announced the opening for settlement of old Oklahoma and many from this area took part in the 26 mi. race to Kingfisher.

John D. Brown was president of The Citizens Nat'l. Bank about 1890.

1889 and others to follow, were disastrous for Kansas businessmen, as well as owners of farm lands. Money became scarce, mortgages were being foreclosed, banks failed, even companies went to the wall and ceased loaning on land.

In 1889 property in town and country depreciated until Anthony became almost bankrupt."

Ferguson

From the "Kansas Cyclopedia" 1912

Ferguson is a station on two railroads, the Kansas City, Mexico and Orient and the Rock Island. It is a market for livestock and grain. The first postmaster was William Kuykendall appointed July 12, 1904. The population in 1910 was forty. The railroads have been taken up, the church disbanded and there is no population. Ferguson was located on Section 25, township 34, range 8 west.

Goss

Giles M. Goss was born in North Carolina, March 21, 1825. He started west when only sixteen living for a time in Indiana where he married in 1842. Next he moved his family to Iowa where he became a successful farmer and stockman. In 1876 he visited Kansas looking for a suitable location. He was so impressed with Harper County that he returned to Bloomfield, Iowa, and organized a colony known as the Goss and Glenn colony, which was composed of eleven families. The colony came west that year and founded the town of Harper. Goss acquired 1,400 acres. On a portion of his land the little village of Goss came into being. He purchased twenty acres from Andy Griesinger on high ground and built a three-story house that could be seen for miles. On this property he planted many, trees and hand dug a well of 80 feet. John Schnackenberg who was a lad at the time tells that Mr. Goss always drove a team of high spirited horses to a fine buggy and would toss pennies to the children along his way.

Neaty and Giles Goss were parents to ten children. Neaty died November 2, 1880, and was buried in Spring Grove Cemetery. In 1881 Goss married Miss Mary Drake. Mary was the first postmaster of Goss being appointed May 24, 1892. (The post office was discontinued September 30, 1896.) Giles died September 7, 1894 and was buried beside his first wife.

Goss was located on the north one-fourth of the northwest one-fourth of section 12, township 34, range 8 west.

Harper

From Andrea's History, 1883

The city of Harper, the oldest city in the county, takes its name from the county. It is located at the terminus of the K.C.L.

and S.K. Railway, ten miles from the eastern line of the county and nine miles north of Anthony, the county seat. The growth of the town has been very rapid and it bids fair to become one of the most prosperous of the many good cities in Southwestern Kansas.

Harper was settled by a party from Iowa, consisting of J. B. Glenn and family, M. H. Glenn and family, R. and A. T. Barton with their families, Joseph Haney, C. H. Snider, M. K. Kittleman, G. M. Goss, C. C. Goss, Thomas Elder, B. L. Fletcher and H. C. Moore. This party came to Hutchinson on the Atchison, Topeka and Santa Fe Railway, and thence, April 2, 1877, struck south to Kingman.

Arriving at this point, they engaged county surveyor Sugars to accompany them to Harper County and locate the town, which should be the future metropolis. Starting at a government cornerstone two miles southwest of Kingman they ran a line due south into Harper County, where they camped on April 5, on section 19, township 32, range 7 west. The next day, a line was run to the east line of the county with a view of locating the town where the railway from the east, that all expected soon. Three surveys were made and the town finally located on April 14. R. and A. T. Barton built box houses on their claims. Both houses were just outside the townsite. The first house in Harper was started April 16, by J. B. Glenn, with lumber hauled from Wichita. This house now serves as the kitchen of the Glenn House. C. C. Phelps put up a blacksmith shop, which was soon followed by the residence of B. L. Fletcher. A town company had been formed while the party was at Hutchinson, and J. B. Glenn was elected President, and C. H. Snider Secretary. April 30, J. J. Merrick came to Harper and soon after procured building material at Wichita and built a house, the front part of which was used as a gorcery. S. S. Sisson who arrived in Harper County in May 1877, was the first attorney in the new county and Dr. C. S. Lloyd, who came in the fall of 1877, was the first physician to practice here. Due to its rapid growth Harper was considered a boom town from 1878 to 1882.

Harper was organized as a city of the third class on September 7, 1880, and the first city election was held on the 25th of the same month. This resulted in the choice of S. S. Sisson, Mayor; G. W. Appley, Police Judge; R. B. Elliot, H. Martin, R. J.

Jones, S. D. Noble and L. G. Hake, Councilmen. G. W. Appley was appointed City Clerk.

On July 1, 1877, Mrs. Jossie B. Glenn was appointed postmistress of Harper, the first post office in the county. The government, although granting a post office, made no provision for mail carriage, and this duty was performed by William Glenn, who made weekly trips to Hutchinson. On July 1, 1878, a weekly mail was put on by the Government and this soon passed through the transitions of semi- and tri-weekly to a daily hack from Wellington. This was continued until September 16, 1880, when the railway arrived and mail service was transferred to the postal clerk. The post office was moved from the Glenn House to the hardware store of Wilson and Baumstack, thence to the present location in the store of J. H. Maxfield. The first money order issued by this office was purchased July 7, 1879, by J. B. Glenn. Daily mail routes from this office run to Wellington, Medicine Lodge, Anthony and Kingman, and a semi-weekly to Wichita.

The first school in Harper was a subscription school taught by Harry Barndollar, in a room over Frank Blackstone's store. H. C. Fulton followed with a subscription school taught in the fall and winter of 1878-79. The first public school was taught by Miss Alice Carpenter, who was the first person in the county to receive a teacher's education and certificate.

The school building, 24 by 60 feet, was built in 1880, at a cost of $1,000. The school had an enrollment of 165 students at the last report which was dated August 1, 1882. A new stone or brick building will be erected in 1883, at a cost not to exceed $10,000.

PRESBYTERIAN CHURCH

The first religious services in Harper were conducted by Rev. A. Axline in 1877, and a Presbyterian church was organized. A church building was completed in June 1882, at a cost of $2,000.

METHODIST CHURCH

The Methodist church was organized in 1878, with a membership of seven, under the care of Rev. J. W. Anderson. Early services were held in private houses and the schoolhouse. The first church was erected in 1882 at a cost of $3,000.

Baptist Church

The Baptist Church was organized in December 1881, with a membership of 15. No pastor has ever settled here, and no regular services held. There is quite a flourishing society (Chikaskia) at a schoolhouse six miles northeast of town. A society of about forty has been collected, and regular services are being held.

The Harper County Times

The *Harper County Times* was the pioneer in the journalistic field of Harper, its first issue bearing the date of October 24, 1878. The paper, which took the form of a six column folio, was published by W. O. Graham. In January 1879 owners were the Graham Bros. On August 26, 1880, ownership passed to Graham Bros. and Finch. The form of the paper was changed January 15, 1880, to a six-column quarto. The *Times* now has a circulation of 550; twice each year special editions descriptive of the county, reviewing its early history, are published. The paper has always advocated the views of the Republican Party.

The Harper Sentinel

The *Harper Sentinel* issued its first publication August 17, 1882. Its editor was W. A. Richards. This publication was of the six quarto form, and supported the Republican banner. December 21, 1882, a careful review of the history of the county and town was issued. February 10, 1883, the paper was sold to O. O. Leabhart, who issues a second special historical number March 1; the paper now has a circulation of 500 and appears Thursdays.

Banking

The first banking house in Harper was that of Wood's, Parsons and Co., which started in 1880. This being a private bank, it makes no public statement of resources, but the fact that Hon. John G. Woods, of Wellington, is a large owner is sufficient to guarantee the stability of the concern.

Thompson and Walton started the second bank in Harper on July 1, 1882. This is a private bank and makes no public statement of its resources.

The Arcade Mills

These mills were completed July 8, 1882, at a cost of $18,000, by H. C. Smeltzer and Co. They have four runs of buhr-stones, and a capacity of seventy-five barrels of flour per day. The machinery is driven by an engine of sixty-five horse-power; the building is of stone 36 by 30 feet, and has three and a half stories.

History of Churches in Harper (city)

As taken from a historical collection of Harper County Churches 1961.

The First Presbyterian Church 1877

In compliance with an invitation the Rev. Andrew Axline visited Harper City, and that time preached to the people the first sermon ever preached in Harper County, in the dining room of Glenn Hotel.

Rev. J. P. Fulton, appointed by the Presbyterian Board of Home Missions, was in charge of this congregation until 1885.

The original frame church building was destroyed by a cyclone in 1893. A new and more commodious church was built on the site. This church celebrated its 75th anniversary in October, 1952. The prospects of the church are very hopeful for a future of youthfulness. The present membership is 160.

The First Methodist Church

The Rev. J. W. Payne organized the church January 10, 1879. He left Mrs. E. S. Morgan in charge until a pastor could be appointed. After walking from Kingman, wading the Chikaskia River at bank full, The Rev. J. W. Anderson arrived March 15, 1879, to become the first pastor.

Services were held in local homes until 1882 when the first local church building was completed. The dedication was held May 4, 1882.

The ladies of the church purchased an organ in 1881 and the first public appearance of the choir was on Sunday, May 18, 1882.

The local paper commented December 28, 1882, "The new bell for the Methodist Church arrived just in time to ring out a genuine surprise to our citizens Christmas morning. It weighs 700 pounds, has a deep, rich, voluminous tone, and seemed to penetrate the atmosphere for miles around."

The final service in the old church was held November 19,

1911, and the new church was dedicated November 26, 1911.

This building served the congregation until the new church was consecrated on April 7, 1968. This new structure is perhaps one of the most modern and beautiful churches in the state.

With the merging of the Evangelical United Brethren and the Methodist organizations on April 1, 1968, the church is now known as the Harper United Methodist Church.

The present membership is 480.

The First Baptist Church

In 1885 plans were completed for the new church, on the present location of the church parsonage. It was completed and dedicated in the spring of 1887. For several years the church prospered and was one of the largest in this community. Many members were lost when the Oklahoma strip opened. In 1930 the old building was razed and construction started on the new church.

The present membership is 40.

St. Patrick's Catholic Church

The St. Patrick's Catholic Church was organized in the year 1882. The church structure was destroyed by tornado in 1892. In 1897 a new church was built on the present location. During the following years the church was remodeled (1939 and 1948).

On July 27, 1948, the Bishop blessed the newly remodeled church. On January 30, 1949, Rev. J. A. Wechensky called a meeting of the church committee for the purpose of considering a resolution pertinent to the incorporation of the Diocese of Wichita. It was considered and unanimously passed.

In 1965 a large and beautifully designed church was built.

At present there is a seventy family membership.

The First Christian Church of Harper

The First Christian Church of Harper was organized in 1880 as the result of a series of services held by Elder A. H. Mulkey. Most of these services were held in what is known as Spencer's Hall. In 1884 a frame building with some remodeling, served the congregation as a sanctuary until the present building was erected on the same site in 1917-18.

There are 200 members at the present time.

The Eastside Church of Christ

In 1945, 35 members of the Eastside Church of Christ met and formulated plans for the building of a new church. Members of the new congregation constructed the building with very little outside help. The building was finished for services in March of the same year. Ordination of deacons and elders was held on June 7, 1945 by Evangelist H. L. Gipson. The membership at that time was 35.

At the present time the membership is 60.

Harper Seventh-Day Adventist

The present day congregation had its beginning February 1903 in the South Rochester School. Later they met in homes of members, the next move was to the Honey Creek School; next they met in the Christian Church in Spivey. Their next move was to worship in the Four Acre public school. Later they met in Duquoin. In 1938 they purchased the Methodist Church in Duquoin and worshiped there until the building became unsafe.

On August 6, 1950, Elders Kirby and Patton began a series of meetings in a tent on West Main Street in Harper. At the close of these meetings it was decided to build a church in Harper. The construction was started in 1951 and was financed by two of the brethren, Earl Cole and Lloyd Carrick.

Harper Assembly of God Church

The Assembly of God Church of Harper was started in June 1951. W. E. Hampton came as pastor and the meetings were held in his home.

In 1952 the congregation rented the hall on North Central. In June 1952 the church bought three lots and a parsonage located at 604 East Main. The church building was started in September 1955 and the first service was held in the new building November 6, 1955.

The United Missionary Church, Harper

(Formerly Mennonite Brethren in Christ. Change made at General Conference at Potsdam, Ohio, 1947.)

The Harper United Missionary Church had its beginning in the last part of the 19th century. One of the first of the young men of the plains to enter the Gospel ministry was Omer B.

Henderson who began preaching in 1894, and that same year organized a church group at Hillsdale, Kansas. A church was dedicated in 1899.

The church branched out to hold services in the communities of Runnymede, Antelope and Grove schools.

In the early days money was scarce, and the ministers had to labor with their hands to maintain themselves and their families. The task of opening up the frontier was far from easy. Most of the pastors had at least four or five appointments. Many of the services were held in small one-room schoolhouses. At times as many as 200 gathered to worship in these small buildings.

Sometimes a minister would receive only one or two dollars in cash during a three month period. The preaching of these humble, consecrated men of God aroused not only interest but antagonism as well.

In 1928 arrangements were completed to move into Harper.

Brother Snyder reported that the work was "a City Church with a Country Congregation."

(Practically the reverse is true today. Virtually all of the members and adherents are residing within the city limits of Harper.)

Pleasant Valley Mennonite Church (1888)

The Pleasant Valley Mennonite Church was organized in 1888. The first Mennonite settlers arrived in 1883. These first settlers came principally from Harvey County, Kansas, and Wayne County, Ohio.

The first services were held in the homes, gathering in time for dinner which was followed by Sunday School, Scripture reading, and occasionally an exhortation by one of the lay brethren.

In 1888 the congregation worshiped in the Pleasant Valley School. The first church building was constructed in 1897.

The original building was replaced in 1915. This building was remodeled some years later.

The present membership is 200.

Their splendid new church was built in 1963.

West Side Church of Christ (1884)

The West Side Church of Christ was organized in 1884. Their present house of worship is full of history. The building was first a two-story structure erected to serve as the county courthouse should Harper become the county seat. After the county seat was settled at Anthony, the building was used to accommodate the Harper Normal and Business College in 1886. After the college had ceased to exist the top story of the building was removed and it became the home of the West Side Christian Church. Today the church has 40 members.

The Topeka Daily Capitol

Jan. 20, 1929

Harper Couple Tell Thrills of Pioneers

Mr. and Mrs. David Wagner, residents of Harper County for more than fifty years, recently recounted some thrilling pioneer experiences when they celebrated their fifty-third anniversary.

They settled two and one-half miles north of Harper in a dugout. There this young mother with two small children remained alone, while the husband, a stone mason, sought work in nearby towns.

Wichita, then the nearest distributing point, the unbridged Chikaskia River lying between ofttimes caused delay and delivery of supplies. Then the sod corn, sown by Mrs. Wagner's own hand, frequently was dried, ground in the coffee mill and made into hardtack for the family food.

The cowboys of the Tripple X ranch once furnished her a good supply of meat for the winter. They were en route to Wichita, driving a large herd to market and camped in a draw near the Wagner dugout. Later, when they dismounted to ask for water, they were so touched by her manifest fear, followed by a courageous attempt at concealment that the foreman assured her there was no occasion for fright.

On the following morning a quarter of baby beef was unloaded at her door and the fat from the entire animal left at the camp for her to gather up, after they had hit the trail.

When Mrs. Wagner was asked for her most thrilling experience, she said:

"It was a night in a drenching rain with owls and rattlesnakes."

She was alone with her baby when gathering clouds frightened her into a night trip to a neighbor's a mile away, where her oldest child was visiting. Gathering up her year-old baby, her only companion, she went out into the dark night, which grew darker and darker, and when she was only a short distance from home the heavens opened and the rain came in torrents. She walked and walked. With no light except the blinding lightning she became bewildered—lost on the prairie.

The human bundle in her arms grew heavy, but she trudged on for hours. Suddenly she found herself in a ravine. In vain she strained her eyes for a dimly lighted house. Exhausted, she stood waiting for a lightning flash which soon came and revealed a nearby buffalo wallow, bordered on one side by a high mound, where she decided to remain for the balance of the night.

Nestling the drenched baby closely, she sank down to await the breaking of dawn, when suddenly a hissing noise mingled with a screech told of her intrusion in the den of rattlers and owls.

Springing up, she stood in another attempt to get her bearings. The storm was beginning to abate. In the far distance she detected what she thought was a light and headed for it. After hours of slippery walking she reached the old Glenn House in Harper at three a.m. with a good foundation for pneumonia, but the baby suffered no ill effects.

An experience of Mr. Wagner's is no less thrilling. He was working in town and the lodging houses became so infested with the early day pests of the new town's bed bugs—that Dave decided to try the hayloft of the old "red barn" on North Central Avenue. Finding no one there he prepared to sleep: the only requisite being a reclining posture, as those were the days when men slept with their boots on and their ears open. Suddenly he heard great talking below. Two lanters were suspended.

A shot was heard, followed by the breaking of glass and the lights went out. Two men rushed from the barn. Soon back to the barn came the coroner and others.

The building and all within was locked up awaiting the coming of dawn. Professor 'of Music' Harness had been mysteriously shot while talking to John Dobbins. A seemingly well-founded suspicion rested on Frank Hayes, a supposed county seat traitor. But one of Lamonyan's boys, of the North Side Town addition, was arrested, tried and found "not guilty." Wagner was interviewed by an attorney and told to go to his farm.

But the red barn took on a ghostly aspect, was soon vacated and torn down.

Mr. Wagner, who now claims an earthly heritage of four children, ten grandchildren and one great-grandchild, says his hair has refused to lay down on his head since that eventful night.

OLD RUNNYMEDE CHURCH

The church once stood in Runnymede, an old English village nine and one-half miles northeast of Harper, along the Chikaskia River. The church was dedicated as St. Patrick's Episcopal Church in 1889, but was re-dedicated in the name of St. James in 1893, when Episcopalians of Harper purchased the frame building and moved it to its present location at 11th and Pine streets.

In 1959, the Episcopal Diocese of Salina, retained ownership of the ground but gave the building to the Harper City Historical Society who undertook the restoration and preservation of the church as a monument to local history. Through donations of materials and labor the outside has been painted grey with white trim. The interior furnishings are for the most part, retained from the Runnymede era. It is certain that the stone baptismal font and bronze memorial plaque were imported from England. The pews, kneeling benches, choir seats and a few Bibles, hymnals and prayer books are among the original contents. Three stained-glass windows, lights, carpeting, organ and altar furnishings have been added since the church was moved to Harper. Artifacts of old Runnymede are housed in the rear of the church. An oil painting of the original town of Runnymede, by Agnes Nye, hangs on a rear wall.

The church is open to the public at scheduled times.

FIRST NATIONAL BANK OF HARPER, KANSAS

From "The Harper Times," June 1, 1882.

"The new Banking House of Thompson and Walton which is now being established in our city is such an institution as deserves at our hands more than passing notice. It is located on Central Avenue in the new building south of the old "Elliott Place" and is a good situation for business. The partners are both young men of ample means and large experience. They own the "Sunny Side Ranch" in the western part of the county on which they have at present 2,500 head of high grade Moreno sheep. They will continue their stock interest in the county as they find it a paying investment."

*   *   *   *

Louis Walton was elected president of the bank in 1882 and served until 1897 when F. R. Zacharias was elected to the presidency. Mr. Zacharias served until 1919 when he was succeeded by Marcel Duphorne. In 1936 L. D. Banta became president and is still serving in this capacity. Mr. Banta received his 50 years of banking service pin from the Kansas Bankers Association.

With 54 years of banking in Harper, Mr. Banta has seen this institution grow from under $200,000.00 to over $4,000,000.00 in deposits.

The first public statement on record issued December 3, 1907 listed assets as $227,115.43. The 1915 statement was $248,775.58. 1917 $435,614.31.

The present officers are: L. D. Banta, President; Elden Clements, Vice President; Angel Esparza, Cashier; M. J. Hooley, Assistant Cashier. The Directors are: L. D. Banta, J. E. Ahlf, W. C. Long, Jr., Elden Clements, C. V. Terrell and Phil Banta, Jr.

THE RAILROAD COMES TO HARPER

In July of 1880, $28,000 in bonds were voted to make possible the advent of the Southern Kansas and Western Railway. Of this amount Harper Township voted $16,000 and Chikaskia Township voted $12,000.

On September 10, the first train steamed into Harper.

In 1902 the Orient came to Harper.

In 1912 the Orient depot burned.

In 1914, one day was declared "Santa Fe" day. On this day the new brick depot, which is still standing, was dedicated. There was a grand parade of autos and ladies in colorful dress.

In 1957 there were 40 trains per day, six being passenger, into Harper.

Today the A.T. & S.F. brings in one train, the "San Francisco Chief."

The Orient was disbanded some time ago.

THE WICHITA EAGLE

Dec. 23, 1923

FIRST CHRISTMAS DINNER AT HARPER, KANSAS, IN 1887 CARRIED OUT DESPITE BIG HANDICAPS.

In 1887 ladies of Harper, Kansas, their hearts starved for companionship, conceived the idea of having a community

Christmas dinner. The plan was carried out and Harper's first Yuletide festivities occurred in the pioneer home of Mr. and Mrs. D. S. Goss, newlyweds, who still reside in that city. They had just arrived that spring by prairie schooner drawn by mules and oxen, from Bloomfield, Iowa, to settle in the new country.

The Christmas dinner presented many obstacles. But the pioneer heart was undaunted. First there was the limitation of the portable larder, transported from Wichita by wagon sixty miles distant. But the dinner was a consuming desire among the women. They took their patchwork for miles on the open prairie to neighbors and thus planned the affair.

A large table was constructed of boxes and pieces of lumber in the sod house of the Goss family. A buffalo committee was named weeks in advance. Judge J. J. Merrick made the arrangements and aided by others he saw to it that a buffalo was obtained. There was plenty of rabbit on hand if the buffalo ran out and the pioneers were well accustomed to eating rabbit. This fare was supplemented by good Iowa canned fruit, the best of which had been saved for such an occasion. And Iowa hazelnuts were perhaps the greatest delicacy of the dinner.

It might be added that after the lapse of nearly fifty years any of the above mentioned delicacies would still be held in much favor in any Christmas dinner of today.

Sugar was very scarce in those days but "black strap" was sweet and sufficed. And there was Kaw "plum pudding" and pressed wild flower decorations.

Mary Morgan, mother of Methodism in Harper, expressed the thanks of these happy-hearted frontier sons and daughters. Those who participated in the never-to-be-forgotten affair were the families of G. M. Goss, D. S. Goss, Evan S. and James Morgan, Joe Haney, Ross Barton and sons, J. B., M. H. and S. H. Glen and son, Robert, Uncle Dick Gorman, and family of four girls, Mamie Haney Thompson and Pearl Glen Robinson, Dr. and Mary F. Martin and the W. W. Kittleman family.

THE ROTHWELL OPERA HOUSE, HARPER

On the evening of June 25, 1884, the Grand Ball hailed the opening of the Rothwell's Opera House, on North Central Avenue in Harper, Kansas. This was perhaps the outstanding social event of all time.

Stanley's Orchestra furnished the music from the large orchestra pit.

The 50 by 90 foot structure was built at a cost of $30,000.00 and another $15,000.00 was spent for extra construction and equipment. The built-up balcony had 15 rows of seats, along with the boxes and general seating accommodated 700 people. Large heating stoves stood in each corner. Gas lighting was used throughout, on stage, and in a massive chandelier hanging in mid-theater. During daytime hours, a mammoth solarium glass dome bathed the second floor interior with natural light.

On August 7, 1884, the Harper Dramatic Troupe presented the four-act drama entitled "A Wronged Wife." Admission 50 cents per person, box seats for six people were $5.00. Other plays included "Uncle Tom's Cabin," "Ben Hur," "Seth Swap" and "Driven From Home." The Georgia Minstrels also appeared in 1884. Professor Martin held a dancing school in the old Opera House.

Many gala occasions were recorded here through the years, then on the evening of May 27, 1892, a tornado inflicted heavy damage to the building. It was rebuilt but never regained the major influence it once enjoyed.

The City of Harper Through the Years

On Dec. 28, 1877, Dr. H. C. Fulton started a private school.

June 1, 1878, a subscription school was opened by Harry Barndollar. The attendance was 40.

April 14, 1879, the first public school was started with an average daily attendance of 40.

June 1, 1880, census—212.

Sept. 7, 1880, Harper was organized as a city of the third class.

Sept. 16, 1880, first railroad arrived.

Sept. 25, 1880, the first city election was held.

Aug. 9, 1883, the first Public Library was organized but was a failure. It was reorganized in 1884.

March 17, 1877, Dr. C. S. Lloyd located in Harper. He was the first permanent physician.

Sept. 22, 1878, the first marriage in Harper was that of Dr. J. W. Madara and Mary Glenn.

Oct. 24, 1878, the first issue of the *Harper County Times* was published. This was the first newspaper in Harper.

April 14, 1879, school district No. 5 was organized.

May 17, 1879, the Harper guard consisting of 80 men was organized to guard against Indian uprisings.

Oct. 1886, R. W. Ball, from the University of Michigan, opened the Harper Normal School and Business College. There were 200 students enrolled.

In 1880 there were two daily and two weekly newspapers in the city of Harper, a bakery, a cigar factory, broom factory, hardware store, two livery stables, two blacksmith shops, a lumber and coal yard and a wagon building establishment. There were also restaurants, ice cream and candy stores. A brick yard was opened and board of trade was organized.

In 1883 the town had three banks.

In the early 1900's there were seven drug stores, five lumberyards, nine grocery stores and two saloons called "blind tigers."

In 1901 the Southwestern Bell Telephone Company came to Harper.

In 1905 the city light plant was built.

The sewer system was constructed in 1912.

In 1914 the Harper College was established on West Main Street. The school grew rapidly and in 1918 was moved to the College addition on South Pine Street. The college consisted of eight grades—four years of high school and four years of college. The girls' dormitory was destroyed by fire in 1924 and the college was moved to Morrillton, Arkansas.

The Harper Study and Social Club built the City Park in the middle 30's and presented it to the city.

In 1953 the swimming pool was constructed by the city.

Harper has a unique landmark. On the water-standpipe jauntily swings a huge fish—to tell the Harper citizens which way the straws are blowing!

Present Day Harper

Modern Harper is to south Kansas what Lindsborg is to all of Kansas. Lindsborg is an older town with a distinct Swedish background having Bethany College and world famed Birger Sandzen as supports. Harper is coming up the hard way, by its own 'boot straps.' Today Harper proudly maintains a thriving art center where its members may paint daily and where they may market their efforts. There is at this time a 'Little Theater' movement. Harper hopes to enjoy summer theater. An art seminar was held in the spring of 1968 with famous people lecturing on many aspects of art.

Harper Cultural Arts Association was founded in 1966. It consists of four divisions: Music, Arts, Theater and Writing. Four piano recitals by faculty artists have been held and at the present time a ballet school is being formed.

The Women's Civic Improvement League was organized in 1966. Physical labor by townspeople, with money donated by private citizens, has built a children's swimming pool, two downtown parks; painted forty benches, fences and buildings. They have also painted the red and white stripped fair barn. The present project is a new fountain to be built at the intersection of the two main streets in Harper.

The Harper Historical Society, Inc., was formed in 1959. One of the first activities of the newly formed organization was the restoration of Runnymede Church and the City Historical museum. Both buildings are open to visitors from 2:00 to 5:00 each Sunday from May through October. Since the opening date the church has had 4,065 registered.

The Museum is one of the most unique in the country. Thousands of items such as a large scrapbook of information about Harper County, pictures, Bible collection, rock collection, broommaking, musical instruments, a country store. Farm implements are displayed here in an unusual manner. Since opening day, more than 3,300 visitors have registered.

Harper, with a population af approximately 2,000 inhabitants, is a thriving agricultural and manufacturing community, located fifty miles southwest of Wichita, Kansas, on a diagonal highway, K-2. It is located on the main line of the A.T. & S.F. railway. Two other highways lead in and out of Harper, K-14 from north to south and US 160 from east to west. In addition Harper has bus service both north and south and east and west. There is a well-kept airport which is available for many types of airplanes. Some of Harper's local businessmen own and operate their planes.

One of the main resources of Harper is a bountiful supply of good water. Electricity and power are available in any quantity for manufacturing and other uses.

Harper has a number of Civic Clubs as well as a Mayor and Council form of government.

The health facilities of Harper are excellent, with a new modern hospital and clinic to serve the community. Harper has a modern well equipped Care Home.

The city is now becoming a center for small manufacturing firms. The most recent being the Slope Tractor Company. Plans are being made to build a new modern factory to house this rapidly growing industry. The company produces tractors used by highway departments and railroads. They are designed to operate safely on steep slopes.

Another manufacturing firm is the Raye Machine Company. Their product is a medium sized hydraulically controlled loader. This loader is known as the "Raymon" and is shipped to all parts of the country.

Harper's fire department is recognized as one of the finest and best equipped in the state of Kansas, considering the size of the community which it serves.

A new City Building is now under construction. This building will house the city offices and the public library.

The Harper Armory houses the National Guard unit in this section. About 70 members belong to this group.

HOSPITAL DISTRICT NO. 5, HARPER, KANSAS

Hospital District No. 5 had its beginning on December 19, 1960, and was formed under the provision of Kansas G.S. 1959, Supp. 80-2178 to 80-21, 100 inclusive at a temporary organizational meeting at the Harper National Guard Armory. The temporary board was named: Robert M. Bolitho, Chancy H. Hostetler, Geo. E. Gleichman, Herbert Mathes, and Carl Sanders. Robert M. Bolitho was elected chairman of the temporary board.

Griffeth and Bonham, Architects, were engaged to present prospective plans to be presented to the District No. 5 eligible voters.

A special bond election was held on April 25, 1961, with 820 'yes' votes and 197 'no' being cast for the new $250,000.00 hospital.

Carl and Harriet Frische donated $25,000.00 to the project. The building contract was let on December 20, 1961.

In October of 1962, the Administrator, Anthony R. Schultz, was hired.

The original staff members were Dr. A. R. Edmundson, Dr. K. A. Bush, Dr. R. E. Bellar and Dr. L. C. Joslin.

The annual meeting held May 3, 1968, reported an income of

$186,363.00 which is a gain of $44,000.00 over the previous
year. There are 33 employees with a 1967 payroll of $102,697.00.

Forest Hoover was reelected to the Board for a second term.
Other directors are Geo. Gliechman, Lee Unruh, Carl Sanders
and Russell Smith.

The hospital is a Blue Cross participating hospital, a provider
of Medicare services, a member of the American Hospital Association and a member of the Kansas Hospital Association.

Dr. Geo. M. Hostetler, M.D., will move to Harper in June,
1968. He will be associated with Dr. Ralph Bellar and the
Harper Clinic.

PRESENT-DAY STATISTICS

The Harper schools are in Unified District No. 361. There
are 414 students in the elementary school and 234 students in
the high school. There are 42 teachers in the present system.

Number of books in the school libraries is 7,308.

Number of books in the public library is 9,666.

The post office is located at Ninth and Central and was built
in 1960. There are three R.F.D. routes from this post office.

Lodges: American Legion, Masonic Lodge, I.O.O.F. Lodge,
Rebekahs, Eastern Star and Order of Rainbow for girls.

Civic Organizations: Civic Improvement Club, Historical So-
ciety, Inc., Cultural Arts, Art Association, Inc., Chamber of
Commerce, Jr. Chamber of Commerce, Lions Club, 4-H Clubs,
Twentieth Century Book Club, Saddle Club, Harper County
Fair Assn., Harper Community Theater, Boy and Girl Scouts of
America, B.P.W., Summer Recreation Commission, Civic and
Study, Study and Social, International Christian Leadership,
and Harper Book Club.

*   *   *   *

Present-day Harper is quaintly picturesque with its wide, tree-
lined, brick paved streets, downtown park complete with grass,
flowers and gaily colored benches. Along Main Street is a white-
trimmed, red converted livery barn. It now houses the annual
County Fair displays and art shows.

A flower-based fountain graces one intersection. One sees
handsome modern buildings along with those of another day and
time. The old Patterson hotel long unused has been reopened by
Roselea, of New York. The old hotel now wears a fresh dress of
scarlet paint.

In the foyer are art objects (weaving) and crafts for sale. You may stay the night and commune with the ghosts of the boys who used to gamble in the undercroft and mingle with the new crowd that is newer than tomorrow.

Inyo

This store and post office was located in the southeast one-fourth of section 6, township 31 south, range 9 west. According to the Harper County Atlas of 1886, the land was owned by I. B. Doolittle. The post office was established on November 7, 1879, and was discontinued February 18, 1893. The first postmaster was Fred Hagaman.

Joppa

This post office bears the name of "Old Site Joppa" in the 1886 Atlas of Harper County. Its location appears to be north-west one-fourth of Section 4, township 31 south, range 8 west, on land owned by Peter Squires. The post office was established June 30, 1879 and was discontinued October 14, 1884. The first postmaster was John A. Squires.

From "The Harper Graphic," July 4, 1884

Ten miles west of Harper the new town of Joppa was recently platted. There they have several stores, blacksmith, stage stand, etc., and there is good opportunity for building up a nice town, situated in Bluff Creek valley.

Odell

The Odell post office was established on August 19, 1878 with Mrs. S. J. Cleous as postmaster. The office was in the Cleous home. The post office was moved to Coleville which was nearby, January 24, 1881.

Coleville

Coleville was the original name of the town of Danville. Coleville was named for Mrs. E. J. Cole who laid out the town. The town company purchased twelve acres and changed the name of the town to Danville. Several of the early residents had come from Danville, Ohio. A number of the people who settled here were French and of the Roman Catholic faith.

The first postmaster of Coleville was Mrs. J. E. Wilson. The office of Coleville closed January 25, 1882 to become the Danville post office.

Danville

Andrea's History 1883

Danville is a live little town, of about 200 inhabitants, located on the K.C.L & S.K. Railway, seven miles from Harper and about the same distance from the east line of the county. The townsite of sixty acres was laid out by Mrs. E. J. Cole in 1880, and a post office known as Coleville established. Of this sixty acres the town company purchased twelve, and made their improvements thereon, the name of Danville being substituted for Coleville. The Town Company's first officers were T. O. Moffett, President; J. A. Burke, Vice President; G. P. Pearl, Secretary; F. O. Mott, Treasurer.

The first building on the town site was a residence moved in from the country by F. O. Mott, the second was the blacksmith shop of E. Mackey, and the third was the general store of T. O. Moffett. This was soon followed by the store of L. B. Ammerman.

The post office, both under the name of Coleville and Danville, has been in charge of Mrs. J. E. Wilson.

The press history of the town is summed up in that of the *Danville Argus.* This paper was started on November 10, 1882, by R. E. Hicks. After two months, it was sold to J. R. Horn, and in February, 1883, it passed into the hands of a stock company. It was started as a Republican sheet but changed to Democratic views upon coming into the possession of J. R. Horn. Its form is that of a "patent" five column quarto.

The first church building in the town was erected by the Presbyterian society in 1882, at the cost of about $800. This is used on alternate Sabbaths by a Methodist society. The Roman Catholics also have many members and have secured funds for the erection of a chapel.

The town now has three grocery stores, one drug store and a

combined drug and grocery store, one dry goods store, one hardware store, a lumberyard, meat market, two blacksmith shops, one livery and one shoe shop. There are two coal dealers and two grain buyers and one hotel.

*   *   *   *

NOTES TAKEN FROM AN EARLY HISTORY OF NORTHEAST HARPER COUNTY.

By Odell Cleous—1947

"The first farm to be broken out in Harper County was the Edward Mackey homestead, two and one-half miles east of Danville.

"The oldest barn standing in Harper County belongs to H. H. Herst, two miles north and one east of Freeport and was built by John Lawson. The lumber was hauled from Wichita in 1879.

"The first school taught in this county was by Miss Amie McDaniel in 1879. Joseph Fisher taught the second school in this district under my kitchen in 1880. (Mr. Fisher was the father of A. Fisher, present County Commissioner of Harper County.)

"In speaking of our barn of 1877, there was one election held there, one dance, and church several times. Many a man looking for a home stayed overnight in this barn.

"The first grain binder in this neighborhood was owned by a man named Young in 1883. It cost $300.00 and used broom wire for twine. This binder was the "Old Buck Eye." The first threshing machine that I can remember was owned by N. G. Baldwin, an old horsepower. It was used for wheat, rye, and millet that was raised here at that time.

"I expect that one-fourth of this township was broken out by ox-team. At one time grass all over this country would grow five feet high. We had some big prairie fires that would jump the Chikaskia River. I know of one fire that came through here that burned 200 head of sheep for Dr. Hetsler about twelve miles north of here. The doctor said that he found out later the fire started in Nebraska and burned south to the Red River, north line of Texas.

"There was an Indian burying ground in my pasture.

"The railroad came to Danville in August, 1880.

"The Danville bank was started in 1905 by Roy Shannon from Attica.

"The first grain header was owned by Bobbie Iriton in this

township in 1880. He worked one team of horses on our side and a yoke of oxen or cattle on the other.

"In 1918, Danville was known as the second largest distributing point in the United States for the Harley Davidson motorcycles. They were sold by Joe and Ed Drouhard.

"The first people who lived near Danville were John Burke and his brother-in-law, William McIntosh, also Theodore Beldin. They came here in August, 1878. Until William McIntosh's death March 1, 1945, he had lived in Harper County longer than any other man, over sixty-seven and one-half years.

"The first white child born in this township and this county was Agnes Jesseph, daughter of Henry Jesseph.

"One of the worst storms to ever hit Harper County was on January 7, 1886. The temperature dropped to 25 degrees below zero. A man living in the Bluff City area lost a herd of Texas cattle valued at $30,000. One steer survived the storm.

"On May 25, 1898 there was a hailstorm that did heavy damage to the farms of John Schon, J. M. Fulton, D. F. Herst, and Henry Greve.

"On May 27, 1892 there was a cyclone near Harper. Our part of the county was severely damaged by hail. Orchards and gardens were a total loss. Our cows were beaten until their backs were bloody.

"In 1895 this country blew away. Many fields as deep as they were plowed. The following year we raised a good crop of corn. My brother Albert and I hauled 100 loads of corn to Argonia and sold to Augstead and Barrett for 16½ cents per bushel. The next February we hauled to Albion and sold for 12 cents per bushel.

"The following teachers have taught at District 25 in Odell Township since November 1, 1878; until the time of its closing in the spring of 1939: Amie McDaniel, Joe A. Fisher, Mrs. Harmon, Fred Beach, Belle Neely, Sam McClure, James B. Curry, John Milford, Lola Bates, Cas. C. Braden, Sam R. Ball, John Fisher, Thomas Elder, Doug Murphy, Ted Schaffer, Sarah Purcell, Oliver P. Dillman, Alice Ruley, R. S. Hammond, Wm. Aldridge, Ralph Gailey, Jacob W. Fisher, Jesse Row, Effie Schriver, Fannie Gilbert, Joe LaPlant, Rephelius Pegram, Zulu Cline, Hazel Watkins, Mary Sisson, Orpha Litsey, Armanda Ellington, Dora Kohling, Laura Bay, Elsie Ford, Mae Ford, Mae Fisher, Emma McDaniel, Leona Wynett, Beulah Laughlin, ? Switzer,

Ruth Wooley, Jessie Bradshaw, Alice Hansbarger, Lucille Rhodes, Nellie Mott, Frances Whistler, Ethel Miller, Hazel Mc-Cully, Mrs. A. Fisher, Helen Kirk, Delphia Phillipi, Evelyn Mc-Clung, Ruth Babcock, Helen Kiner, Marie Oliver, Sallie Hill and Helen Jesseph."

*   *   *   *

From *The Danville Courant*,
May 19, 1883

The new Catholic church at this place had its cornerstone laid last Sunday with the lengthy and imposing ceremonies of the Catholic church ritual. The structure is to be 36 feet wide, 50 feet long, the walls 18 feet high. Father Kelly of Winfield conducted the ceremonies and deposited a sealed package containing an inscription in English with the name of the Pope, the Bishop, the President of the United States and the name of the church—St. Rose of Lima—inscribed thereon together with a copy of the "Danville Courant" and some coins of the present time, were sealed by Father Kelly in the cornerstone in the presence of a large concourse of people.

*   *   *   *

Notes from "A Historical Collection of Harper County Churches."

"According to information given to us, a few Catholics settled around Danville, Kansas, in 1880. They came from Danville, Ohio. During the construction of the church, mass was held once a month at whatever place was available; once in a drug store, in a harness shop, in the residence of Mrs. Colopy, also in a schoolhouse. Mass was even said in the Methodist church. By 1902 the congregation had grown until a new and larger building was needed. In the fall of 1903 the old church was moved and was made into a school and the foundation for the new church was laid. On June 3, 1904, the name was changed from St. Rose of Lima to Immaculate Conception Church. The new church was completed and dedicated on November 21, 1907, by Rt. Rev. J. J. Hennessey."

PRESENT-DAY DANVILLE

The present population of Danville is 90. The post office is located on Main Street in a building erected in 1932.

The Roman Catholic Church with a membership of 375 serves the community.

There are two lodges, K. of C. and M.W.A.

The present business establishments are two grocery stores, two grain companies, service station, blacksmith shop, seed cleaner and repair shop.

Otego

The village of Otego was located three miles north and three-fourths east of Crisfield. The legal description being northeast one-fourth of section 4, township 33 south, range 9 west. According to the 1886 Atlas of Harper County the land belonged to O. C. Hooker.

Ira Crow, now of Anthony, was born near Otego. At that time there was a store and post office. The storekeeper was a Mr. Rankin. A woman M.D. had an office there. She ushered Mr. Crow into the world.

The post office was established November 23, 1882 and was discontinued February 27, 1885. The first postmaster was George W. Clark. The post office was moved to Crisfield.

Ruella

Ruella, located on the Missouri Pacific Railroad now has only a small country elevator. The first postmaster was Branson Jackson, appointed July 17, 1884. The town was served by four passenger trains per day and there was a large depot with a platform as high as the passenger coaches. There was a store, blacksmith shop and several residences. The location of Ruella is west one-half of the southwest one-fourth, section 15, township 34, range 8 west. The post office was closed May 31, 1889.

Ruby

Ruby was a small village whose post office was established on May 13, 1902; the postmaster being Leonard K. Belding. Mr. Belding also operated a store and blacksmith shop. There were a few residences in Ruby which was on the Rock Island Railroad.

This was a favorite spot for Sunday baseball games. The post office was discontinued in 1904. Very little remains of Ruby. Its location was the east one-half of northeast one-fourth of section 13, township 34, range 8 west.

Runnymede (Old Runnymede)

G. W. Francis, a native of Ohio, came to Kansas from Illinois in March, 1877. He took a claim in the original Chikaskia Township. The legal description being the northwest one-fourth of section 7 and the north one-half of the northeast one-fourth of section 7 all in township 31 south, range 5 west.

Since Mr. Francis took 240 acres and planted 600 forest trees and 50 fruit trees we would presume that he was operating under the provisions of the Timber Culture Act of 1873. The Act offered 160 acres to anyone who would plant 40 acres in trees and maintain them for ten years. It has been estimated that about 4 percent of the public lands in Kansas were taken in this manner.

After living at this location for over two years, the Runnymede post office was established on his land, June 20, 1879, and he was appointed the first postmaster.

G. W. Francis, Civil War veteran, and Kansas pioneer was a prominent factor in the development of Harper County. He became an extensive farmer and took an active part in local politics. He was a lifelong Republican and at one time, represented Harper County in the State Legislature.

While improving his land, he was not forgetful of the educational needs of his own children or those of his neighbors. A school taught by his daughter, Miss Eva Francis, was held in his home—tuition free. This we believe was the first school in Chikaskia Township.

In the 1880's Francis J. S. Turnley came from England and bought 1700 acres along the Chikaskia River. The original village of Runnymede was in this tract and as far as can be determined, was used as the nucleus for the Runnymede which became Harper County's most colorful bit of history.

"They Had a Good Time while It Lasted"
RUNNYMEDE, KANSAS, 1889-1894

From "International Finders"
By Virginia Sharp Hooper and Agnes Nye

— It all started when Francis J. S. Turnley came from England around 1880 and later bought hundreds of acres along the Chikaskia River, north and east of the town of Harper.

"Ned Turley's idea was to recruit a colony of English sons of wealthy families to whom he would teach the gentlemanly art of farming and help them to buy land. His proposition was publicized in England as 'a western paradise where golden birds sang in the trees and silver rivers ran tinkling to the sea. The climate is so healthy it puts to shame any reference to Elysian Fields.' He promised the farming would be a good outlet for youthful exuberance. For this service, he asked a fee of $500 per man. He did outfit many with ponies and saddles, but probably never did teach farming as he was essentially a promoter. English communities in America were being settled; his was not unique. There were two others in Kansas and one at Rugby, Tennessee.

The Englishmen who responded to this scheme were largely remittance men—second sons of wealthy families, who were often shipped off to colonies to alleviate by distance their scapegoat escapades. The family back home would remit monthly a sum in pounds sterling to maintain the expatriate in a suitable fashion. Their thoroughly British nature, their fun-loving, carefree attitude, and their wild exuberance at being free of Victorian atmosphere of England burst onto the frontier like water released from a broken dam.

After stumping about England advertising his plan, Turnley returned and built a barracks, called Chikaskia Ranch, and sat back, with Capt. Wood, Capt. Faulkner, and Col. Filliter, to await the first boatload of settlers. The *Britannic* of the Red Star Line, sailing on May 29, 1889, brought sixteen men and women including two of Turley's three sisters. Figures vary as to whether the peak population was 85 to 100 or up as high as 200, including some Kansans who joined the fun.

The next man of importance in the story, perhaps even more important than Turnley, was Robert W. Watmough. He was a dashing horseman, a popular man in his twenties, the life of the party. His significance was that he was the one who actually thought of founding a town, of laying out streets, building up commercial and residential property, and incorporating as a town. He gradually bought out Turnley, promoted numerous interests, carried at least one through to a profitable success—the soda water factory. In fact, Turnley resorted to the one remaining business—promoting a railroad through the town—for this he sold bonds. Watmough wrote a column in the *Harper Sentinel* about the activities and the social life of Runnymede, signing himself the "Bird of Freedom" and buoying up the spirits of the displaced Englishmen with such gay exclamations as "Verily the town boometh!" and "We are a happy family! We are! We are! We are!" Watmough's activities as a town developer came to a head in January of 1889, when the first store opened. Eighteen ninety was the peak year. The church had forty members, the hotel was continually filled with guests. Hopes were great that the railroad would come through town. Then tragedy struck.

On May 14, 1890, our hero was guest of honor at a ball at the Runnymede Arms before his return to Ireland to marry Hilda Turnley, who had been in Runnymede and had returned to Ireland. That night he slept in the community barn and a fire started. Watmough may have started it himself by smoking, for the fire raged out of control and Watmough lost his life. He was buried in Harper at the age of 23. The tolling of the church bell signalling the last rites for him carried an ominous prophecy in its somber tones. It was the sounding for the death knell for Runnymede. The town lingered on a number of years but its soul was gone. They soon learned that the railroad was a loss, too, and general financial troubles of the 1890's finished off the venture. By 1895 most of the buildings had been moved away.

The former residents of Runnymede went to various places, some to Harper, others to England and at least one to Mexico.

So this is a short tale of Runnymede. We will list some of the individuals who lived there and the institutions and customs of the settlement.

Major John Lobb was best described by Major Seaton: "Who could forget him? He was the beau of the steeplechase. He once wore a white stiff bosomed shirt, a collar and flowing black tie, alpaca coat, checked trousers halfway to the knees, white sox, dancing pumps, ranger hat, and lavender kid gloves. He was a poor rider, could hardly keep his seat and at the finish his head was at a 45° angle while his legs were around the horse's neck."

H. G. Hoblin tried to farm, but could not resist the lure of the chase, banquet, ballroom, so weeds overtook his farm. He traded part of his land to Col. Todhunter of Lexington, Missouri, for a stable of race horses and polo mounts. Hoblin's mother and sister arrived from England for a visit. He purchased a new carriage and a pair of high-steppers to meet them at the train in Harper and frightened them with his ugly dirk and six-shooter.

The Nye family, (family of W. W. Nye of Harper) had three generations in Runnymede at one time. Abraham Nye was born in England, married in Pennsylvania, raised five sons, then moved to Kansas, settling at Turnley's ranch about 1888. He took care of the horses and his wife, Mary, cooked for the ranch. His son, Whit Wilson Houser Nye and his wife Mary Alice, came there with nine children of whom Agnes Nye's father-in-law, William McClellen Nye, was the second and twelve years old. He set pins in the local bowling alley. About 1890 the Nyes lived in Runnymede. Two Nye brothers came to the community. Henry D. Nye, who ran a steam laundry a short while and Abe and Lillie Nye.

The race track opened on October 10, 1889. All races were held with frivolity and fanfare and were more noted for enthusiasm than for ability of racing. The town boasted a steeplechase course, a fairly good stable of polo ponies and race horses, polo games, foxhunts, and carriage races.

The tallyho began its run to Norwich and Harper in the fall of 1889, though little heed was paid to schedules. A trip meant to take four hours would often turn into a ten-hour detour before the passengers were finally deposited in a riotous manner at their destinations. It was an old-fashioned stagecoach driven by four horses. The Runnymede folks rode on top. The bugler blared a long trumpet, or sometimes the whole band played music, folks sang songs of old England.

The commercial enterprise in Runnymede had its inception in Turnley's realization that nearby merchants were growing fat on business from the Runnymede folks. To cash in on his captive source of revenue he set up a commissary at his ranch. Watmough bought out Turnley and relocated the commissary on the west side of Main Street with a new sign "Watmough General Merchandise Store." Following this, there appeared a hardware store, a nursery, a livery stable, green grocery, drug store, creamery, billiard parlor, bowling alley, lumberyard, soda water factory, art gallery, the church and the hotel and a blacksmith shop. A restaurant was brought from Norwich and served until the hotel was opened, then was converted into a laundry. In the middle of Main Street was the town well. Watmough started ventures, then sold out to various citizens. Turnley had actually lost out by this time, however he continued to go to England for new colonists.

St. Patrick's Episcopal Church was dedicated on November 21, 1889 by Rev. Dr. Beatty of Wellington, Kansas, as the first St. Patrick's Episcopal Church in America. The interior furnishings were largely imported from England, including the baptismal font and bronze plaque. It still has three of the original beautiful stained-glass windows and the original pews, altar, and choir seats. In 1891 it was finally located at 11th and Pine in Harper where it has received proper care from the Harper Historical Society and was redecorated in 1960. Glass cases at the entrance display some of the old Runnymede photographs.

The Runnymede hotel was moved to Alva, Oklahoma, and in 1960 was still serving the public under the name of "Runnymede Hotel." The third floor has an interesting wood railing encircling the center stairway. The top gables were destroyed at some time by fire, but it still has three stories.

From the "Runnymede Items,"
Signed, the "Bird of Freedom"

"The first wedding took place at the English colony on Saturday, February 22, 1890, at St. Patrick's Church, the high contracting parties being Miss Sophia Dorothea Turnley, daughter of John Turnley, Esk., I.P.D.L. of Drumnasole, Antrim County, Ireland, and Percy, A. E. Wood (of the Titippo Stock Farm) late of York and Lancashire Regiment, son of Col. O. Wood of the Indian Staff Corps. A wedding breakfast was held at Ned Turnley's ranch. The wedding cake which was from Messrs. Buzzard & Co., London, England, was of surpassing magnificence. About 3 p.m. the far famed white steeds of the Runnymede livery barn were brought round to the entrance hall and the bride and bridegroom entered the chariot amidst the good wishes of the crowds assembled. Some of the presents are listed below: F. J. S. Turnley—thoroughbred horse; the boys of Run-

nymede—handsome antique oak writing table; Mr. Dick Watmough—Mexican mustang hair bridle and bit."

After all, the venture was but a flash in the pan. The sounds
of bugle and thundering hooves have died away, a vague pat-
tern of the racetrack remains refusing to allow the farmer's wheat
to obliterate the evidence of sight, sound, and gaiety of a time
now cataloged in the eternities.

Runnymede (South Runnymede)

According to old Atlas maps South Runnymede was located
nearly one mile south of the original town post office. When the
location was changed the post office was taken to the new location. With the revising of townships (Harper and Chikaskia)
South Runnymede was found to be located in Harper Township
with the legal description of southwest one-fourth of section 12,
range 6 west. South Runnymede was platted in a four block
area with the Kansas City, Mexico and Orient Railroad passing
through the town. It may be assumed that the coming of the
railroad was the reason for changing the townsite.

Shook

The village of Goss faded away and in 1900 a new town
grew in its place with its name changed to 'Shook'. This new en-
deavor was on the Missouri Pacific Railroad. For a number of
years this was a thriving trade center with a general store, depot,
blacksmith shop and several residences. The first postmaster of
Shook was Jesse Montgomery and the office opened July 27,
1900 and closed November 18, 1900 but the order was rescinded
and Shook was again in the postal business June 1, 1901 and did
not close until July 15, 1925. At this time only a grain elevator
remains. The school, one mile west of Shook, now discontinued
was called Goss School.

Bill Barber who bought the land on which Goss had stood
said, when he started the new town, "We shook the name of
Goss so we'll just call the new town 'Shook'."

Sonora

The Sonora post office was located in the southwest one-fourth of section 12, township 34 south, range 6 west on land owned by A. Culbertson. The Atlas map (1886) shows Sonora as being situated in a large grove of trees, probably a timber claim. The post office was established March 8, 1880 and was discontinued May 25, 1888. The first postmaster was Azariah Culbertson.

Sullivan

The United States Postal Department lists this post office as having been located in Harper County, but the exact location can not be determined. The Sullivan post office was established December 15, 1885 and was discontinued June 19, 1886. The first postmaster was Shelton Morris.

Swan

Mr. T. D. Hunt of Rural Attica states that many years ago a post office and saloon were located approximately nine and one-half miles west of Anthony. Mr. Hunt could not recall the name of the station. This could have been Swan but there is no official record.

The Swan post office opened December 5, 1879 with Daniel V. Hamilton as postmaster. The office closed February 27, 1880.

Waldron

The city of Waldron, Harper County had its beginning, according to an abstract of title issued to H. B. Waldron for Sec. 15, Twp. 35, R 8 W on the 6 p.m., Lot 1, compiled by Roscoe R. Beam, bonded abstracter, Anthony, Kansas. The legal entry according to the abstract, Lot 1, east of the townsite proper, was deeded to W. N. Myers by the United States government. Date of the instrument being Dec. 2, 1879, and filed Sept. 29, 1880, the consideration being $40.00, recorded in book A, page 221. The amount of the land being 40 and 10/100 acres. This is the earliest record of land transaction in this particular area. The town proper was placed on Lot 2. A free patent was granted to Harrison Latham, Nov. 20, 1880 for Lot 2, Sec. 15, Tws. 35, R 8 W. This grant was for 40 and 30/100 acres. Book A., page 219.

It is well to note that these parcels of land were in the original Cherokee Strip.

On Sept. 5, 1880 W. M. Myers sold his tract to LaMont C. Bidwell for a consideration of $250.00, recorded in book B, page 232.

On Aug. 9, 1882 Harrison Latham sold Lot 2 to LaMont Bidwell for the consideration of $150.00, book D, page 23.

Bidwell deeded this land to Howard B. Waldron, Jan. 23, 1892.

The following is taken from an agreement dated Dec. 17, 1901. "Party of the first part between Union Real Estate and Townsite Company, a corporation and party of the second part, J. A. Stine, trustee for the Choctaw Northern Townsite and Improvement Company, and party of the third part, H. B. Waldron, Anthony, Kansas, agrees to transfer and dedicate for townsite purposes the following described real estate situated in the county of Harper, state of Kansas, to wit: All the portion of Section Sixteen (16) lying east of main line and right-of-way of the Kansas City, Mexico and Orient Railroad. Also a strip of land forty-four rods wide (East and West) off the West side of section Fifteen (15) and adjoining section 16. All of said real estate being in Township thirty-five (35) South, Range Eight (8) West of the 6th Principal Meridian, containing 140 acres, more or less, EXCEPTING, such portions of said real estate as is now occupied by the Choctaw Northern Railway for right-of-way purposes, also such real estate as may hereafter be conveyed to the Kansas City, Mexico and Orient Railroad Company for station facilities under terms of this contract. . . . also said party of the third part shall construct upon said townsite, at a place to be designated by the Board, a 'Town Well' with two tanks and proper equipment, at a cost not to exceed two hundred and twenty-five dollars ($225.00). . . . And parties of the first part hereby agree to procure the Kansas City, Mexico and Orient R.R. Company to erect on said townsite of Waldron, Kansas, a station on said townsite within ninety days after they have laid rail into and through said townsite. . . . both parties of this contract are equally interested in the establishment and building up of the townsite of Waldron, Kansas, at the crossing of our respective lines in Harper County, Kansas, and to the establishment of a good and prosperous town on said townsite, free from the rivalry now existing between Camchester and Manchester O.T. and other towns in the territory of Oklahoma, we hereby contract and agree that none of our trains shall be permitted to stop at any station or townsite within a distance of seven miles (7) south of the townsite of Waldron, Kansas."

According to the abstract Howard B. Waldron platted a strip of land, 726 feet east and west off the entire west side of Section 15 in Township 35, south of Range 8 W in Harper County. This plat and other lands to be known as Waldron, Kansas, April 15, 1902. Recorded in book C, page 20.

Howard Waldron on contract, exchanged the townsite plat for property in Kansas City. The exchange was made with W. A. Rule, Feb. 18, 1903.

W. A. Rule sold the property to G. T. Bomgardener on Mar. 15, 1904 for $1.00 and other considerations.

G. T. Bomgardener sold the property to L. A. Sharrard on Mar. 25, 1904, consideration, $4237.50.

Nov. 1, 1905 the office of the Secretary of State granted a charter to the Waldron Townsite and Reality Company. Seven directors were chosen, stockholders being the same.

J. W. Harris, Nortonville, Kansas.........99 shares
S. O. Harris, Nortonville, Kansas......... 1 share
W. B. Collett, Atchison, Kansas..........99 shares
A. H. Collett, Atchison, Kansas........... 1 share
L. A. Sharrard, Meriden, Kansas.........98 shares
M. R. Sharrard, Meriden, Kansas........ 1 share
A. C. Cutler, Waldron, Kansas........... 1 share

The estimated value of the corporation is $3000.00 and shall be divided into 300 shares at $10.00 each.

In searching the files we find that a second town charter was issued Aug. 25, 1913 by the Secretary of State, Charles H. Sessions. The Directors under the new charter were as follows:

J. W. Harris, East Las Vagas, New Mexico
L. A. Sharrard, Kansas City, Missouri
Marry Sharrard, Kansas City, Missouri
W. B. Collett, Atchison, Kansas

L. E. Johnson, Waldron, Kansas
N. E. Johnson, Waldron, Kansas
L. E. Krider, Waldron, Kansas
The stockholders under the second charter were as follows:
J. W. Harris, East Las Vagas, New Mexico . 50 shares
Susan O. Harris,
    East Las Vagas, New Mexico . . . . 49 shares
L. A. Sharrard, Kansas City, Missouri . . . . . 98 shares
Mary Sharrard, Kansas City, Missouri . . . . . 1 share
W. B. Collett, Atchison, Kansas . . . . 49 shares
Annie H. Collett, Atchison, Kansas . . . . 50 shares
L. E. Johnson, Waldron, Kansas . . . . 1 share
N. E. Johnson, Waldron, Kansas . . . . 1 share
L. R. Crider, Waldron, Kansas . . . . 1 share
The value of the corporation remained the same.

> Files for the preceding information
> were furnished by Mr. Herb
> Snyder, Anthony, Kansas.

WALDRON

The town was platted in a forty-seven block area. Some of the early businesses were: two hotels, a drug store, two saloons, two grocery and general stores, two livery stables, two blacksmith shops, two hardware stores and a machinery dealer. There were two newspapers, *The Waldron Argosy* and *The State Line Democrat*.

The water tank and windmill were on Main Street. The Kansas City and Orient depot was located in block 12. The Choctaw-Northern depot was in block 14, on Orient Street.

The community supported a three-room elementary school.

There are three tax supported cemeteries in Eagle Township.

PRESENT-DAY WALDRON

The town of Waldron now has a population of 25 and is in the unified district (school) #361.

Present-day business houses are grocery and service station operated by Myrtle Welch. There is a repair shop and service station.

The post office is under the guidence of Flossie Bettis who has served in this capacity for 25 years. Aubry Harrison is the R.F.D. carrier.

WALDRON CHURCHES
Assembly of God

The Church at Waldron was started in 1931 when revival services were held in a tent. After the revival a building was rented. The church was organized in April 1938. The church was first called the "Pentecostal Assembly of God," but, in 1941, the name was officially changed to the "Waldron Assembly of God." In 1940, the building the church had been renting was given to them as a gift at the death of the owner, Mrs. Bassitt.

The present membership is 25 with Rev. Johnston as pastor.

The Christian Church (1932)

The church building now known as the "Waldron Christian Church" was built in 1903 by the United Brethren. Mrs. Waldron, mother of Howard Waldron, founder of the town, donated a large part of the cost of the building. After several years the Congregational people bought the church building and held services until 1932. The Christian Church was organized in 1932 with 25 charter members. Once more the little church building took on new owners and a new name.

Yankton

Yankton, a pioneer village in Ruella township opened its post office Aug. 6, 1883. Postmaster was Stephen C. Oliver.

The *Yankton Gleaner,* an eight page, eight column paper was devoted to the interest of Yankton and vicinity. Subscription rate, $2.00 in advance. The post office closed Oct. 14, 1884.

Business Directory

The Yankton Literary Society meets every Monday night at 7 o'clock. S. C. Oliver, president, L. A. Jones, secretary.

Wilson Risley, Attorney at Law, office on the south side of square.

Joseph Brockway, M.D., office in the center of Rizelbrocville.

Wm. Brockway, Dentist. Office over Dr. Brockway's, all work warranted.

The Yankton Hotel. Also in connection, a Livery, Feed and Sale Stable, S. C. Oliver, Prop.

A. J. Barr, Plasterer, Bricklayer and Sod Carpenter.

R. S. Sullivan, Shoemaker and Cobbler. All work warranted not to rip, tear, or run down at the heel.

L. A. Jones, Hair Dresser. All work done on the European Plan. A cold bath in connection.

Marcus Oliver, Real Estate, has a number of city lots for sale cheap. Also running a peanut stand in connection, north side of square.

SPRING "TENNESSEE" TOWNSHIP

The story of "Tennessee" Township is one of interest and color. William H. Burchfiel came to Harper County, Spring Township, from eastern Tennessee in the spring of 1878. He left behind a brother J. R. "Parson" Burchfiel who was a circuit rider in the hills of Tennessee.

William sent glowing reports back to the old home. "Come to Kansas," he wrote. "This new land is the answer to our prayers." In turn "Parson" Burchfiel persuaded others to join him.

After much planning and consideration a party of forty adults and children, was organized to make the long journey to Kansas. Early on the morning of January 28, 1884, they gathered on the banks of the French Broad River, where a large flat boat was to take them to Knoxville. After singing the hymn, "Shall We Gather at the River," the Tennesseans bid farewell to their home and friends.

The party chartered a rail coach from Knoxville to St. Louis. On arrival at St. Louis there was no transportation between railroad stations. This weary group presented a colorful sight as they trekked across the city. Each person was traveling on a full fare ticket which allowed him to carry 250 pounds of baggage. Imagine this caravan of men, women and children walking through St. Louis loaded down with bundles of all shapes and sizes, baskets of lunch, valises of clothing and almost everyone carrying a sack over his shoulder filled with seeds, fruit, grain, and nuts, all of which would be so necessary in establishing their new home.

(Author's note) In interviewing Callie Burchfiel of Anthony, he was asked if he had heard the above story, "Heard it? Well, I guess so, I was there. I squalled all the way across St. Louis. I was just a little shaver and had fallen against a hot stove, both hands were burned, yes, I was there alright."

When they arrived in Harper Uncle Billy Burchfiel and others met them with teams and wagons and brought them to the Tennessee Settlement.

William H. Burchfiel who located here in 1878 worked especially for the interest of his fellowmen and might truly be called the founder of the Tennessee colony that established itself in Harper County. Burchfiel Church, Spring Township High School, and the substantial farms and homes of the Burchfiel community are a living monument to the ideals of William H. Burchfiel and his brother "Parson" Burchfiel.

"Parson" Burchfiel who influenced the building of the Burchfiel Church served as its minister for many years. He also donated the present Burchfiel Cemetery site.

From *The Anthony Republican,*
May 19, 1938

"Parson" Burchfiel always spoke extemporaneously, but did put in writing one sermon which took four hours to deliver—on the subject of baptism. Miss Gavetia Burchfiel, his granddaughter, is in the possession of this discourse in the "Parson's" own handwriting. She also owns a notebook of hymns, many of which were composed by him and used when he was a circuit rider in eastern Tennessee.

*   *   *   *

The following are two letters written by Flora Russell Nelson. Mrs. Nelson's grandparents were of the original Burchfiel Colony.

Kansas City, Mo.
Aug. 13, 1967

Dear Mr. and Mrs. Sanders,

I received your letter asking if I could give you any information on Harper County, Kansas. My grandparents were Abbegail Margo Reneau and Malcom Campbell McGaha. They moved to the "Tennessee" Colony, about eight miles south of Anthony in February, 1900.

I will give you the story of the Reneaus coming to Harper County. My Uncle Jaques Reneau bought a section of land there in 1884. It was about ten miles from the Oklahoma territory. (At that time it would have been the Cherokee Outlet). An older sister of Abbegail's, Mary Anne Reneau, married her second cousin John Reneau in Logan, Louisiana, at the close of the Civil War and they moved to Dandridge, Tennessee, where their six children were born.

In 1890 Jaques Reneau, now of Harper County, went to Dandridge, Tennessee, to make up a wagon train to come out to Kansas. Aunt Mary and Uncle John Reneau sold their plantation and bought covered wagons and mules and joined the wagon train bound for Harper County, Kansas. About fifty other families from this part of Tennessee made up the train.

Some of the outstanding families in the Burchfiel community were Wes Reneau Burchfiel and his sons John Robert and Frank, and a daughter Evie, who married Mel Henderson.

My parents were Rita Reneau and W. C. Russell. I married Howard Nelson in 1912. He was manager of the Anthony Salt and Ice Co. at that time. My father was a building contractor and built many of the old homes in Anthony.

The thing that brought many of the Tennesseans to Harper County was the prospect of the opening of the Cherokee Outlet. They could obtain land in the "Strip" and still be close to their Kansas homes, the Burchfiel Colony being about nine miles from the state line bordering the Outlet. My aunt Mary Anne made the run and got a good claim near Manchester, where she made her home. However she maintained a dress-making and tailoring business in Anthony driving a horse and buggy thirty-four miles each weekend to her home. She made bridal gowns and groom's suits for many of Anthony's early weddings.

When Harper had its first Fair and Horse Racing Meet my grandmother Abbegail McGaha and grandfather Malcom McGaha, opened their home and fed all the visitors.

Here is a story that you will enjoy: Frank Firestone and Mel Hoopes were merchants in Anthony in 1904. This is the way Frank Burchfiel always told the story, as he was an eyewitness, he always got a big laugh when he told this one. Frank Firestone was a man always ready to help his friends and customers and since it was against the law to sell whisky in Harper County he would go to Kansas City, Missouri, quite often and buy supplies for his big store and he would also bring back a supply of whisky. Cary A. Nation decided to visit Anthony and clean the place up. She spoke at the First Methodist and Baptist churches. Cary got wind of the whisky at the Firestone and Hoopes store and decided to use her hatchet. It was a cold day and in she marched with some of her followers. Men were gathered around the stove and Cary and her crew made for the back room and started in with her weapon, the hatchet. Mel and Frank grabbed her; Mel held her across his knees and Frank spatted her across the rear with a small coal shovel.

Enough for this letter.

I remain,
Flora Russell Nelson

Kansas City, Mo.
Oct. 23, 1967

Dear Mr. and Mrs. Paul Sanders,

You asked about Anthony's salt works. My husband was foreman of the Anthony Salt and Ice Company when we were married in 1912. He started there in 1910. I believe the man who discovered salt was P. G. Walton. The head man of the salt works was Clyde Simmons. John Clinton was on the rake for years.

While visiting in New York recently my daughter reminded me of a story that her grandfather had told her. I will try to piece the story together for you. We had come to Anthony in 1903 at wheat harvest time, for a visit. My cousins had large wheat fields and wanted my father to ride down eight miles on horseback. Some of the men were shocking wheat in one of the fields when my father arrived. My father saw a man that he recognized and said, "Hello, Cal." The man acted as though he didn't know my father. Father knew that this man was Cal D— of Jefferson, Tennessee. Cal had come from a good family but he was the black sheep. Cal's sister and her husband owned a nearby farm. Since coming to Harper County, he had married and had a little boy. He used the name of Frank Jones. While in Tennessee, Cal had belonged to a gang of bank robbers. The cashier of the last bank job had been killed. Father said that he had learned later that Cal's brother had put him in a box and drove fifty miles in a covered wagon and put the box on a train. The box was addressed to his sister in Anthony. Frank Jones lived the rest of his life as "Frank Jones, good citizen."

My father felt grief for the young wife and little boy so he kept the secret until after the death of "Jones" and then he only told me and my children.

I hope that I have helped you.

Flora Russell Nelson

*   *   *   *

THE RUNAWAY DEPOT

As told by Mrs. Callie Burchfiel
nee-Nellie Temple Bettis

Life in Spring "Tennessee" Township was good. Many interesting things happened. Perhaps one of the most exciting incidents occurred when I was but a child on my way home from school.

The railroad had built a depot on the siding north of our home hoping that a town would build close by, with Anthony on the north, Cameron on the south and Bluff City to the southeast. This new town failed to develop, so the depot was loaded on a flat car for shipment to another point.

Cameron was the focal shipping point for local cattle and cattle brought up from the Outlet starting their trip to the eastern markets. The train would not make a trip down unless there were at least 1,000 head to be shipped.

During the loading and switching the steam engine ran low on water so it was decided to go to Anthony for a fresh supply.

In the meantime a strong north wind had sprung up and for some reason the flatcar loaded with the depot started from the siding onto the main line into the path of the returning train. They met head-on, knocking the engine off the track and splintering the depot. It was three days before the wreck was cleared and the cattle loading was resumed.

THE OPENING OF THE CHEROKEE STRIP

Cherokee Outlet (Strip), Sept. 16, 1893

CHEROKEE STRIP OPENING AN UNFORGETTABLE DRAMA

From *The Wichita Beacon,* Sept. 18, 1955,
By Frank Madison, Jr.

"It happened at high noon. The last of the dramatic 'free-for-alls' dashes for homestead land—the opening of the Cherokee Strip on Sept. 16, 1893—has had another anniversary and it seems fitting to glance back at that never to be forgotten American saga.

"The Cherokee Outlet (Strip) is a strip of land approximately 57 miles wide from north to south and extending from the Ninety-sixth westward to the One-Hundredth meridian which is about 165 miles. Its northern boundary being the south line of Kansas.

"Prior to the opening of the Strip large cattle ranches had been established in this area, with the cattlemen leasing these grazing lands from the Cherokees. In 1883, to obtain better terms, the cattlemen formed the Cherokee Strip Livestock Association and made a five-year lease with the Indians for a half million dollars with $100,000 a year to be paid in advance.

"At the end of the first year period another lease for a like term was made, however at an increase in price. The Government frowned on these leases claiming that whatever title the Indians had to the lands, they had no rights to make grazing contracts or leases. Consequently before the expiration of the second lease, President Harrison on Feb. 17, 1890, issued a proclamation ordering the cattlemen to clear the Strip of cattle by the first of the following October.

"Thus ended the cattle ranch business in the Cherokee Strip. What had been the greatest grazing section of like size in the world would be turned into homes for thousands of people from all sections of the United States who already looked with longing and wistful eyes toward the promised land.

"The Cherokees, thus deprived of their source of revenue from the cattle companies, and under pressure from Congress to yield their lands for homestead settlement finally, in Dec., 1891, after much negotiation, agreed to the sale to the U. S. Government of more than six million acres of land located in the Cherokee Outlet for the sum of $8,595,736.12.

"Following the sale agreement preparations were soon made for the opening of the lands to homestead settlement. Congress enacted the necessary legislation in March, 1893; and on Aug. 19, 1893, President Cleveland issued his proclamation that the lands of the Cherokee Outlet including the Pawnee and Tonkawa reservations would be thrown open for settlement on the sixteenth of the following September.

"The lands of the Strip had previously been surveyed during the years of 1872-73. The railroads already had routes across the Strip prior to the opening with the Santa Fe entering from Arkansas City in 1885, followed by the Rock Island in 1888 from Caldwell.

"There had been three land openings in Oklahoma before the Cherokee Strip; however a new feature had been devised for the Strip opening. Secretary of the Interior Hoke Smith, in an attempt to prevent soonerism or making a claim illegally prior to the official opening, made a requirement of all persons desiring to enter a homestead or a town lot must appear at a registration booth and procure a booth certificate certifying he was eligible to enter and file on the land. The age requirement was 21 or over.

"There were nine of these booths, located as follows: just south of Arkansas City, south of Hunnewell, south of Caldwell, south of Kiowa, north of Stillwater, north of Orlando, north of Hennessey, and one between Kiowa and Caldwell (this was Manchester) and one on the south side of the strip near the west end or in Range 26.

"There was reserved for the erection of these booths and for the use of the intended settlers, a strip of land one hundred feet wide within the Strip on which persons might enter for the purpose of obtaining certificates.

The booths were of canvas furnished by the Government, and in each were clerks sent out from the General Land Office at Washington equipped with blank certificates, seals, etc., to be used in the registration. There were two kinds of certificates, form D and form F, the former entitling the holder to make a homestead entry, the latter to file on a town lot."

Kansas Historical Marker (Kansas Historical Society)
(Located three miles south of Arkansas City on U.S.-77)
Opening of Cherokee Outlet

"At noon on September 16, 1893, more than 100,000 people lined the borders of the Cherokee Outlet listening for the pistol shots that started one of the world's greatest races. The prize 8,000,000 acres of land: a quarter section or a town lot to every eligible settler who could stake a claim. For weeks home-seekers and speculators from all parts of the country had been gathering to make the run from this vicinity. Jockeying for position as noon approached were bicycles, covered wagons, buggies, ox teams, Indian ponies and race horses. Thousands prepared to walk and other thousands filled the cars of special railroad trains. When the pistols were fired the mad rush began along the border. By nightfall the Outlet, which for centuries had been the home of the Indian, the coyote and the buffalo, was a settled land of townsites and homesteads."

An interesting story of the "Run" is told about Elizabeth Brennen who had come west from St. Louis.

On Sept. 16, 1893 she made the run into Oklahoma from the Manchester starting point. She made the race in a buckboard accompanied by her future father-in-law, Oscar Bassett.

The pistols had been fired and the great race was on its way. With wheels, horses and miles flying, Elizabeth and Oscar felt the sweet flush of victory. Suddenly there was a great jolting and the sounds of splintering wood. When the horses finally came to a standstill there were but three wheels left on the buckboard. One wheel was broken to bits!

Elizabeth was not to be outdone, she sprang to the ground and seized one of the broken spokes and drove it into the ground announcing that this was to be her claim!

A job in a law office in Enid was awaiting her so by commuting between her homestead and her job she proved her claim.

In 1893, Elizabeth and Floyd L. Bassett were married. They made their home in Anthony and were progressive citizens taking part in the city's first venture in furnishing electricity for the city.

Adelaide Bassett Mahler of Anthony is the daughter of Elizabeth and Floyd Bassett.

Wichita Eagle, Sept. 2, 1953
By Corb Sarchet

"The old Cherokee Strip extended westward all the way from the old Indian Territory western boundary to Texas Panhandle and from the state of Kansas south to the northern border of Payne, Logan, and Kingfisher counties and the Cheyenne-Arapaho Indian country which had been opened in 1892.

"Many years before the Cherokee Outlet was opened for white settlement the government of United States surveyed the present state of Oklahoma and used the usual government method of such survey, which divided the land into townships, ranges, sections and smaller descriptions.

"The only markers to guide the settlers were the section and half-section corners established when the government survey was made. There was a cornerstone or stake at every corner of every section, with markers thereon indicating the number of section, township and range. Each half-mile across the state half-section numbers were established on each section line, but no stake or marker of any kind was set in the center of the section.

"When the Cherokee Outlet was purchased by Uncle Sam from the Cherokee Indians, in order that it might be opened for settlement, the price was $8,300,000 with an additional $300,000 to be paid immediately for the Cherokees and $110,000 to be paid to the Tonkawas and Pawnees for any infringement on their reservations within the Strip. The area opened totaled 5,698,140 acres. In that area now are the counties of Alfalfa, Grant, Garfield, Harper, Major, Woods, Woodward and Pawnee and most of the counties of Kay and Noble and a portion of Ellis.

"Uncle Sam paid the Indians at the rate of $1.50 per acre for the Outlet. Then when it was opened for settlement, each homesteader was supposed to pay $1.25 an acre for his quarter section. A few years later Dennis Flynn of the territorial delegation in congress along with Joe Cannon enacted the 'Free Homes' bill which cleared the homesteaders' land of debt. This act applied to other Oklahoma areas that opened before the Outlet."

THE WEAVER BOYS MEET A HORRIBLE FATE

Retribution   *Harper Graphic,* April 21, 1886

THE WEAVER BOYS MEET A HORRIBLE FATE

Shot to Death — Forty Bullets in One Body

A GHASTLY SCENE

About 11 o'clock yesterday news came that the Weaver boys had fallen into the hands of the avengers and had suffered the death they had so often escaped by the vigilance of the officers.

We hurried to the telephone office and were told that the wires would not work. We instantly divined that it must have been the work of the mob. It was afterwards found that the wires had been cut about midway between here and Anthony.

Finding it impossible to get full particulars, we hastened to Anthony to see for ourselves the extent of the work.

As we approached the schoolhouse where the bodies lay, the most heart-rending cries were heard. On entering the building a scene presented itself that was so horrible as to baffle description. In a corner of a room upon the unfinished floor lay the mangled bodies of the three Weaver brothers—shot to death by the avengers of Dell Shearer. Kneeling there beside them, with alternate prayers and imprecations were the mother of all and the wife of Oliver, while standing by with white faces and mute lips were the father and two surviving brothers, Jake and John. It was a scene that no one could ever forget. The resolute and strong-willed mother was completely broken, and as she knelt at the side of her dead sons and prayed for the vengeance of God upon the heads of those who had done the bloody work, and as shriek after shriek from the lips of the young wife rent the air, the stoutest heart could but quiver, and the strongest face blanch. The white bloodless faces and open ghastly wounds exposed to view were so horrible that one could scarcely bear to view them.

Sick at heart we hurried away to find the sheriff and from him and from other eyewitnesses of the horrible affair we gleaned the following particulars in reference to the shooting.

Our readers are familiar with the shooting of Shearer about two months ago at Danville by the Weaver boys, Phil., Ol., and Hank. At the time it was only with the greatest difficulty that the boys were kept out of the hands of the mob by the sheriff and deputies, and were finally taken to jail at Independence. On last Monday the sheriff brought them back to Anthony for trial and they have been held there since. It was supposed by all that the excitement had entirely abated and that they were perfectly secure. On Sunday night the prisoners were at Sheriff Couch's house, and were guarded by Sid King, one of the deputies. Couch gave Sid orders to wake him about two o'clock to guard till morning. At one o'clock Couch was awakened by King bursting into the room exclaiming, "Ike, the mob is coming!" Couch answered, "Take the boys and run. I will be with you."

Couch's house stands about one hundred yards from the new school building. The masked mob was approaching the house from the front, east, and King went out the back door with the boys and made a run for the schoolhouse. A part of the crowd, who were approaching from the south, saw the run and opened fire, at the same time, Couch, half dressed started to follow them when he was surrounded in an instant, shot at once or twice and a shotgun loaded to the muzzle placed at his head while revolvers glistened on all sides of him. He was quickly disarmed and being heavily guarded was taken to the schoolhouse and compelled to become a witness to all that followed.

Sid King had succeeded in getting into the basement with the prisoners before anyone was shot. He had in his hand a five chambered 45 caliber revolver, but this the boys took from him soon after entering the basement.

The schoolhouse is unfinished, the walls and roof being up and about one third of the floor is laid in each room. At the south side where the boys entered there is a cellar about eight feet in depth, and under the remainder of the building the basement is from three to four feet in depth. To the center of this the boys hurried as soon as possible, while the crowd surrounded the building.

The crowd attempted to procure lanterns with which to light up the basement, but failing in that they began to build fires under the floors by putting straw in at the windows and firing it. All the time a constant fusillade was kept up, shots being fired in at the windows, doors and other openings, while a guard was placed around the block upon which the school is located so no one could approach. Several citizens were captured and placed among the mob to prevent an attack from without, but as the sheriff and deputies were in the hands of the mob no organized interference was attempted.

The sheriff was marched into the cellar in front of the crowd to keep King or the boys from firing. He called upon King to come out, as to attempt to stay in the basement and attempt resistance meant sure death.

After King and Couch were both out, the shooting began in earnest. The fire bells were rung and near half the town was aroused out. The inside of the building was lurid with basement fires and the constant crashing and roar of the guns and revolvers and the shouts of the mob made a scene so terrible that every spectator was thrilled with horror.

The boys had concealed themselves in the center of the northwest wing, and there they met their fate. Ol had taken the revolver from King and had emptied the five chambers with such effect that those who were near say that two of the attacking party were carried to a wagon and hauled away, while some one was heard to remark as one was carried by, 'He is either dead or dying.' Who they were or how badly hurt, of course, will never be known unless one should die.

Volley after volley was fired into the basement, some at random and some when the fires would reveal the hiding place of the victims. The boys stayed together from the first and their bodies were within a few feet of each other.

When the crowd entered the building the boys were found lying partially under the half-constructed floor of the center wing, and near the west wall. Ropes were placed around the necks of all and they were pulled up on the floor. It is doubted if the ropes were used in bringing them up, as none of the knots were tightly drawn. Then the final scene was enacted. About twenty guns and revolvers were fired together making a report that shook the building and the earth around while the flash lighted the whole inside of the building. They then retired to the outside of the building, the word retreat was given and in a few moments there was not one of the avengers to be seen.

A horrible sight met the gaze of those who entered the building. Lying half naked upon their faces on the half finished floor were the bodies of Hank and Phil, almost floating in their own blood, while upon his face on the ground below them lay Ol, still grasping in his lifeless hand the empty revolver that had been powerless to save him.

In the bodies of all were found shot of all sizes. In the body of Ol were found four bullet holes; Hank had received seven bullets besides the shot wounds, while Phil had twenty-two distinct body bullet wounds besides twenty in his limbs and a load of buckshot in his back that had literally torn a hole in his body. Hank had a shot in the back of his head that had blown his brains out and must have killed him instantly.

The mother and wife had witnessed nearly the whole scene and were of course frantic with grief, but were kept from approaching the house by the guards. Mrs. Weaver said that she recognized three of the attacking party.

Thus has ended one of the bloodiest tragedies that has ever been enacted in the west. Of the cause that brought it about none can ever know except those who have lived for years in the vicinity of the Weaver farm and have known their work. The sheriff informed me that he counted forty-one of the mob and he thought there were fifty to sixty of them.

When so many men from one community unite in an act so terrible as this they do not do it without the most urgent reasons. Add to this that they had had two months to ponder this act and its effect and it would seem that it was impossible that it should have been done unless it was justifiable, if such an act can be.

"The Anthony Republican", April 23, 1886

Dr. McAdams of Danville was telegraphed at an early hour. He arrived here at 3 o'clock p.m. and declined to act on the case, but requested justice Blackburn to act in his stead, who at once empanelled a jury composed of the following gentlemen:

I. B. Forbes, P. C. Firestone, Dr. C. E. Bowers, S. E. Adams, W. S. Cade, and W. P. Olmstead.

The jury, after hearing testimony returned the following verdict:

State of Kansas

Harper County, SS

An inquest, holden at Anthony, in Harper County, on the 19th day of April, 1886, before me, A. R. Blackburn, a justice of the peace of the city of Anthony, in said county, on the bodies of Phillip Weaver, Oliver Weaver and Henry Weaver, these lying dead by the jurors whose names are hereunto subscribed,

and said jurors, upon their oaths, do say: That the said Phillip
Weaver, Oliver Weaver, and Henry Weaver came to their
deaths on the morning of the 19th day of April, A.D., 1886, in
the city of Anthony, Harper County, Kansas, by means of
leaden balls, and shot, fired at and into the bodies of said Phillip
Weaver, Oliver Weaver and Henry Weaver, from rifles, revolvers and shotguns, held in the hands of persons, from the evidence
adduced before the jury, unknown, supposed to be an effort to
avenge the shooting of one Adelbert Shearer.

Jurors:
I. B. Forbes
Dr. C. E. Bowers
P. C. Firestone
S. E. Adams
W. S. Cade
W. P. Olmstead

After the inquest was held, the remains of the men were removed to the Adams building, across from the Montezuma
Hotel, where they were taken in charge by the members of the
family present. They were neatly dressed and placd in elegant
caskets. Here they remained during the night. The funeral took
place Tuesday morning from the building mentioned and a
large concourse followed the remains to the Anthony cemetery.

THE CAUSE

The cause of this unfortunate affair is about as follows: On
the 12th day of February Henry Weaver went to Danville and
made himself very obnoxious—wanted to fight, said he could
whip any d—n s— of a b— in the town. He finally encountered
Dell Shearer, and forced a fight with him. Shearer gave him a
drubbing. The next day Phillip, Sr., John Henry, Oliver, and
Phillip, Jr., went to Danville hunting for Dell Shearer, and good
citizens say that several of them were armed with revolvers, and
that they made a public offer of five dollars to anyone who
would produce Dell Shearer or tell them where they could find
him. But he was not there. Phillip, Jr., Oliver, and Henry went
to town again on the 22nd of February, and the following statement made by Dell Shearer, when he was supposed to be on his
deathbed, will show what took place that day:

State of Kansas
Harper County, SS

Adelbert Shearer, being duly sworn, deposes and says, and believing that this is his dying declaration:

Between Neely & Johnson's the Weavers, Phillip, Hank, and Ol, and as I understand, one of their cousins drove up close to the side of my wagon when Henry Weaver said to me: "You've got to either fight me or I'll shoot you right here today," and then I told him to just keep away from me and let me alone. I drove out into the country with Henry Iriton and stayed until I thought they had left town, then I came back to town, as soon as the Weavers saw me they followed me up and called me "sons-of-bitches," each and every one of them swore they'd either whip or shoot me, that I had to fight or they would shoot me. I told them to go away and leave me alone. They kept following me up, when the fracas began by Phil Weaver shooting at me. I then drew my revolver and shot at him, the same instant Oliver Weaver shot me through the left hand. Then Henry Weaver, as he came past D. P. Coles scales, grabbed two of the largest weights and threw and struck me in the left side with one of them. It stunned me and knocked me down. As I fell, Phillip Weaver shot me here in the left side above the hip bone, it lodged near the naval in front, but was cut out by one of the doctors. I got shot four times, five places instead of four. Phil Weaver shot me in the side. The first that Oliver made was through the left hand. I can't tell you who made the other shots, but I believe they all had revolvers and used them. When I fell, being knocked down by the weight, Henry jumped on to me and then Phillip Weaver shot me. That was the first time we came together. I can't tell you how many shots I fired. I dropped the revolver and it will show for itself. I wouldn't be positive that Henry Weaver had a revolver but I think he did.

This took place Monday, February 22nd, 1886, in Danville, Harper County, Kansas. I don't know whether I will get well or not. I haven't much hopes. I believe that I am on my deathbed and I believe that I am as near death as any one can be and still be alive. Yes, I believe I will be punished hereafter, after death, according to the deeds done here. There was no provocation that I know to cause them to do as they did.

Adelbert Shearer

Witness to the above being read and signed:

A. J. McAdams, M.D.
W. E. Butcher

State of Kansas
Harper County, SS

The above and foregoing declaration of Adelbert Shearer was written by me as made by said Adelbert Shearer, and was read over to him by and after being signed by him in the presence of A. J. McAdams, M.D., and W. E. Butcher, he solemnly swears that the declaration as above, to which he subscribed his name, is the truth and nothing but the truth, and that he does this with the full realization that he is about to die, so help him God.

William N. Green
Notary Public

(Seal)

Commission expires Aug. 1, 1887

*   *   *   *

By way of explanation in regard to our new school building, it is well to state that it is constructed of brick with stone foundation. The walls are up and the roof is nearly completed. The workmen have just commenced to laying the floor. There are no windows or doors in the building proper or basement as yet, and the floor beams and partition studding are not enclosed, so that from any direction the greater part of the immense interior can be seen. The shower of bullets that came through the open windows and doors went whistling among the timbers in every direction. Bullet holes in the earth floor of the basement, the masonry, the heavy timbers of the casements are visible everywhere, and many spent balls have been dug out by relic hunters. On the east side of the basement the upper part of the window casings are burnt from guns which belched their deadly shower of lead into their interior.

HARPER COUNTY AGRICULTURE AND WEATHER

When the first settlers arrived in Harper County it was apparent to them that this land was some of the best to be found in the plains area. The eastern part of the county has suitable soil to raise almost any crop the farmer wishes to plant; while in the western part one finds top grazing land. The numerous streams furnish sub-soil moisture for the growing of sorghums for winter feeding.

Harper County is a producing county, winning many farm awards, being the first district in the state to receive a citation for outstanding work by the State Association of Soil Conservation Districts. They have won the Goodyear Tire and Rubber Company award twice and have been runner-up several times. A number of individual farmers have won state and national recognition.

In the last decade Harper has been listed with McPherson, Sedgwick, Thomas, Ford, Finney, Barton, Reno, Sumner and Dickenson as leading wheat producing counties.

The Harper County Agriculture Report, 1886

	1881	1882	1883	1884	1885
corn—					
	22,253 A	23,227 A	27,210 A	31,376 A	44,500 A
	30 bu. A	40 bu. A	50 bu. A	49 bu. A	50 bu. A
winter wheat—					
	7,423 A	8,010 A	11,346 A	20,530 A	23,333 A
	11 bu. A	24 bu. A	23 bu. A	11 bu. A	15 bu. A
oats—					
	no report	718 A	2,688 A	6,490 A	11,538 A
		40 bu. A	50 bu. A	50 bu. A	52 bu. A

The following is a page from the Harper County Commissioner's records: assessors meeting, 1894.

The following basis of assessment was adopted.

stallions, thoroughbred $600.00
stallions, graded 300.00
horses, no 1 .... 90.00
horses, ordinary 60.00
plugs and ponies 24.00
mules, no. 1 .... 90.00
mules, no. 2 .... 60.00
mules, 2 yrs. and under 3 .... 45.00
mules, 1 yr. and under 2 .... 30.00
mules, 6 mo. and under 1 .... 21.00
cattle, 1 yr. 6.00
cattle, 2 yrs. 9.00
cattle, 3 yrs. 18.00
cows, no. 1 .... 12.00
cows, no. 2 .... 9.00
steers, 3 yrs. and over 30.00
jacks, no. 1 .... 600.00
jacks, no. 2 .... 300.00
sheep, no. 1 .... 3.00
sheep, no. 2 .... 2.00
hogs, per pound .... .03
organs 50.00
pianos 75.00
pleasure carriages, no. 1 .... 60.00
pleasure carriages. no. 2 .... 21.00
farm wagons, no. 1 .... 42.00
farm wagons, no. 2 .... 15.00
gold watches 24.00
silver watches 12.00
wheat, per. bu. .... .30
corn, per bu. .... .24
rye, per bu. .... .30
barley, per. bu. .... .30
ice, per ton 3.00

Farm implements were left to the judgment of the assessor. All other property left to the judgment of the assessor. Basis for all land was fixed at $500.00 per quarter section.

Meeting adjourned, Sine Die. E. P. Pennoyer, Secretary

J. B. Linning, Chairman

Attest. Wm. Duffy, County Clerk

The *Anthony Republican* and the *Anthony Bulletin,*
May 20, 1948

HARPER COUNTY RANKS HIGH IN AGRICULTURE

Harper County dairy herds entered in the Dairy Herd Improvement Association consistently rank among the top herds in the state. This probably is due to the high mineral content of the soil, the climate and quality of alfalfa produced in the county.

Harper County is the home of nationally known Brown Swiss and Holstein herds. Outstanding herds are located in Harper County.

Hatching eggs from Harper County are in great demand all over the United States because of their high percent of hatchability. The Thurman and Hoopes Hatcheries of Anthony ship hatching eggs and baby chicks all over the United States. Producers of hatching eggs receive a premium for their eggs. Egg trucks are now picking up eggs at the farm in many parts of the county. Harper County ranks high in turkey production.

The beef industry is also well developed. There are several purebred herds of Herefords, Angus and Shorthorns.

Harper County has been noted for its production of high quality early spring lambs. Over twenty carloads of top quality lambs are marketed each year through the cooperative sheep shipping association. The county is a purchasing spot for purebred ewes and rams.

The soils of Harper County still retain a high percentage of their original soil minerals as evidenced by the fact that the average yield of wheat was 20 bushels per acre in 1946.

Harper County ranks high in the production of high quality alfalfa seed. Harper County received $36,482 from the sale of seed during 1945.

Harper County's basic industry is agriculture and it ranks high among the counties of the state as an agricultural county.

Old-timers say that there has never been a complete wheat crop failure. During the last thirty years the average yield per acre of wheat has been above ten bushels per acre 25 times. During 1945 the acreage and value of farm crops was as follows:

	Acres	*Value*
Wheat	255,000	$6,274,000
Corn	1,100	19,000
Oats	17,920	198,000
Barley	2,600	36,000
Grain Sorghum	8,770	154,000
Forage Sorghum	12,470	196,000
Alfalfa	8,300	185,000
Wild Hay	540	5,000
Total Crops Produced ..		$7,067,000

A MIGHTY GOOD STORY

From *The Anthony Republican,*
October 5, 1906

Dear Editor,

I beg to submit to you the following figures which is the income from 15 acres of alfalfa on my farm in Harper County and an investment of $420.00. We bought 70 head of hogs at a cost of $300.00 which we turned into the 15 acres of alfalfa. These hogs were bought in May and June, 1906. In addition to the pasture they were fed about a bushel of corn per day. On August 1, we separated 23 head and put them by themselves in another part of the field; we fed them corn for six weeks and sold the 23 head for $253.40, leaving 47 head of the original stock which represented a cost of $46.60. At the present time these hogs are worth $568.80, in addition we have 60 head of pigs worth at least $100.00, also 30 tons of alfalfa hay that will sell for $240.00. We have fed these hogs 300 bushels of corn at 40 cents per bushel. We still have pasture enough to last until frost. This operation has shown a net profit of $680.20 from 15 acres of alfalfa and an investment of $420.00.

Yours truly,

H. C. Conner.

Harper County organized the Soil Conservation District June 2, 1945. The minutes of the meetings of this organization reveal to us a regular program of soil conservation and improvement. The following figures are taken from "Farm Facts," a report of the Kansas State Board of Agriculture for 1966.

There were 936 farms in the county: 853 were producing

wheat; 563, sorghum; 16, corn; 449, alfalfa; 489, cattle and calves; 184, milk cows; 122, hogs; and 343, chickens.

The total acreage of wheat sown was 225,000; 216,000 harvested for an average of 24 bushels. Total bushels, 5,184,000 having a farm value of $8,707,300.00

There were 16,000 acres of sorghums planted with 15,500 acres harvested. Grain sorghums harvested were 6,500 acres with an average of 26 bushels per acre for a total of 169,000 bushels per acre having a farm value of $180,300.00.

There were 400 acres of corn planted with an average of 30 bushels per acre having a farm value of $4,300.00.

There were 5,000 acres of oats sown with an average of 27 bushels per acre with a farm value of $80,000.00.

There were 11,400 acres of barley with an average of 30 bushels per acre having a farm value of $292,200.00.

There were 8,400 acres of rye sown with 1,680 harvested with an average of 14 bushels per acre having a total farm value of $23,700.00.

There were 620 acres of soy beans harvested with an average of 11 bushels per acre with a total farm value of $19,000.00.

There were 13,700 acres of alfalfa hay harvested with a total production of 20,000 tons, valued at $556,200.00. There were 900 acres of wild hay harvested with a total value of $24,800.00.

The number of dairy cows in Harper County was 17,000 with a value of $340,000.00; beef cattle numbered 57,300, value $7,047,900.00.

Hogs numbered 3,700, valued at $150,800.00.

Sheep numbered 12,000, valued at $207,500.00.

Chickens—150,000, value—$142,860.00.

The total value of milk produced was $579,200.00.

The value of chickens and eggs produced was $719,760.00.

The Harper County farmers are enthusiastic about the future. At the present time they are joining with Sumner, Kingman, Pratt and Baber counties in an application for a Resource, Conservation and Development Project.

The Anthony Republican and *The Anthony Bulletin,*
May 20, 1948

DISASTROUS STORM AT HARPER, MAY, 1892

The greatest disaster in Harper County's history occurred on Friday evening, May 27, 1892, when the north half of the county was swept by a cyclonic wind, followed by rain and hail. As a result, five persons were killed, forty injured, 60 houses were destroyed, and 4,000 acres of nearly matured grain was destroyed by hail. This was the result of a cyclone, and irresistible straight blow, covering a tract six miles wide. Hailstones skirted its outer edges, old-timers say. The persons dead as a result of the cyclone were William Stranahan; Mrs. Thomas Gallagher, the four-year-old son of Mrs. Gallagher; Louis Harrison; and a child of Mrs. Howard Tomlin.

Pioneers of the Crystal Springs community say that their town was a mass of ruins.

The cyclone struck the town of Harper about 7:15 p.m. The force and fury of the wind was terrifying and its effects terrible. The business part of the town was entirely unroofed; tin roofing was rolled up in wads and scattered over the prairie for at least two miles northeast.

The fine "opera house block," costing about $30,000 had its rear walls crushed in, the roof stripped and upper story wrecked, the chairs scattered everywhere and the walls badly crumbled.

Numerous other destructive storms have been recorded since that time but none so damaging as that of Harper. A tornado which struck east of Anthony September 14, 1930, left in its wake a trail of destruction and damage amounting to thousands of dollars.

Two years later, on June 18, 1932, Anthony staged an enforced municipal housecleaning necessitated by the ravages of a wind storm of cyclonic proportions which hit the city late on that night, causing damage conservatively estimated at $50,000.

The wind, attaining a velocity of almost 80 miles an hour, struck the city about 7:45 p.m. and this phase of the storm was followed by a heavy downpour of rain. When the storm abated the streets were filled with debris—trees, broken limbs, boards, shingles and other wreckage. A number of plate glass windows in the business district were broken, and several windows in the courthouse.

Severe Hail Hits Harper, May 31, 1967

Harper residents took cover as tornado sirens wailed. No tornado hit the town but it was bombarded with hail which accumulated to nearly 10 inches in some places. Nearly all the windows and roofs were shattered and shredded.

Newsum Floral Greenhouse was a mass of broken glass and plants were ground to bits and buried beneath a sheet of ice. Gardens were pulverized.

Harper County road crews were quick to aid city crews with road graders to clear streets of the cover of ice.

RURAL CHURCHES IN HARPER COUNTY

One of the especially gratifying experiences in researching Harper County was visiting the rural churches. We began to understand why Harper County grew to be the great community that it is, rich in spiritual strength to withstand the vicissitudes and grace to remain humble amid countless blessings.

In Harper County we found the most generous people of our experience. Few were too busy to "sit and talk a spell."

The rural church is passing from many parts of our nation but may they remain long with you; urban life is moving in fast and rural life is changing.

Harper County, may you ever keep your wonderful charm and continue to be a people of beautiful hearts.

The following is a verse that we found among rural church histories. Its quaintness, simplicity and sincerity give a glimpse of these God fearing people.

> We love the little Country Church
> Where Christ is still upon the throne;
> Let's keep her altar fires ablaze
> 'Till He returns to claim His own.

(United) Burchfiel Methodist Church (1883)

The Burchfiel Church really began in the late 1870's when Mr. William H. Burchfiel conducted a Sunday School in his home. In 1883 the Burchfiel schoolhouse was built and the people of the community asked Rev. Wood of Anthony to meet with them to organize a Methodist church. The charter members were: William H. Burchfiel and his wife Sarah, George Burchfiel, Mrs. Elizabeth Cary, Allie and Josie Cary and Mrs. Ellen Hager.

In 1884 J. R. "Parson" Burchfiel and his family came to the community. "Parson" served as minister to the congregation for many years.

In 1892 Burchfiel was joined to the Bluff City charge and for twenty-nine years each church had preaching services on alternate Sundays.

In 1902 the first church building was completed and dedicated.

When the parsonage was built in 1921, Burchfiel became a separate church with a full-time pastor.

In April, 1936 the church building was destroyed by fire, in a short time the church was rebuilt.

At this time one pastor serves the Burchfiel and Bluff City churches. The minister is Rev. David Fanshier.

The present membership of the Burchfiel Methodist Church is 102.

Chikaskia Baptist Church (1880)

The Chikaskia Baptist Church, is located four miles east and three miles north of Harper, Kansas.

The first meetings were held in a sod shanty, but organizational plans were not made until February, 1880. There were 15 charter members at that time. The Rev. Moses Parker was the first preacher.

In 1892 the first church home was built. Lightning struck the church in 1938 and it was completely destroyed. A basement was completed April, 1939 which was used as a meeting place until the present sanctuary was dedicated on June 5, 1949.

The present membership is 200 with Rev. Donald E. Welton as minister.

Hopewell Presbyterian Church (1887)

The pioneers of the Kansas plains, living south and west of Anthony, met to worship God in three schoolhouses: Goss, Bluff Creek and Blue School. In 1887 the Hopewell Church was organized in the Blue School house or Beaver College. The need for a larger building was apparent and in 1892 a new and larger building was erected and dedicated as a Cumberland Presbyterian Church.

In 1913 the church became the "Presbyterian Church, U.S.A." and dropped the name of "Cumberland." In 1958 the Presbyterian Church U.S.A. united with the United Presbyterian Church and is now known as the Hopewell United Presbyterian Church.

Between 1920 and 1924 a community house and gymnasium was built. A six-room parsonage was built in 1917.

In 1949 the one-room church was transformed into a modern building with basement and well-equipped classrooms making it an outstanding religious training center.

Among present-day members may be found many descendants of the courageous pioneers who founded this church. Finances depended entirely on farm income. Some years were lean, others were rich but the church continued to grow. The Lord's work is marching on in the Hopewell Presbyterian Church.

The present membership is 83.

Crystal Springs Mennonite Church

In 1890 there were twelve Amish Mennonite organizations in Kansas. Of these Crystal Springs is the only one that has survived as an individual congregation.

The origin of the Crystal Springs congregation was in western McPherson County. The church was located sixteen miles north and four east of Hutchinson.

When the Amish Mennonite settlers arrived in central Kansas there was only an occasional house on the prairie, and most of them were made of sod. Prairie chickens were numerous, and antelope were frequently seen. Land was cheap. The rich, black soil was purchased as low as six dollars per acre.

A church was built in 1884. Pete Miller, carpenter managed the project. He also made the pulpit and benches. These are still being used in the basement of the Crystal Springs Church.

The Amish Mennonites came to the Crystal Springs vicinity after the opening of the Cherokee Outlet. Mortgaged land had been abandoned and was bought by the newcomers.

Late in 1904 the church in McPherson County was dismantled and the lumber hauled to Hutchinson to be shipped by rail to Harper County. The benches, pulpit, doors, windows and frames were hauled by wagons, a distance of eighty-five miles.

The church was rebuilt on a site one-fourth mile east and three-fourths mile south of Crystal Springs. The land was donated by Jonas Yoder.

Important dates in the church history are:

1. 1900—First series of evangelistic meetings.

2. 1920—The Amish Mennonite Church of Crystal Springs merged with the Kansas-Missouri Mennonite conference, thus dropping their Amish affiliations.

3. 1955—Congregation accepted Overseer plan.

4. 1928—New church erected, debt free at time of dedication.

5. 1952—Parsonage was purchased in Crystal Springs.

In 1945 there were 140 members.

As of 1968 the Reverend Mr. Earl Buckwalter and his good wife Rose, minister to the spiritual needs of this courageous and wonderful people.

There are 78 members in this congregation.

CAMP GROUND

OR

THE MYSTERY OF THE CRISFIELD MILITARY INSTALLATION

This has been the most thought-provoking portion of "The Harper County Story." Early in our research we received a letter from Mrs. Lillian Hollister Shaw of Canadian, Texas, asking us to not overlook her beloved Crisfield in writing the book. In her letter she had inclosed a copy of an "Anthony Republican" newspaper clipping, it was a historical discourse written by Mrs. L. N. Hubanks. The article among other things, discussed an encampment of soldiers located southwest of Crisfield in the 1880's.

Many letters and interviews followed. The archives in Washington, D.C., and the State Historical Society in Topeka wrote to say that they had no record of there ever having been any military installation in Harper County.

All of the people with whom we talked who had personal knowledge or a family story of this encampment associated "Indian Scare" with the encampment.

Ira Crow of Anthony had vivid recollection of his parents telling of 1500 soldiers being stationed at the Crisfield site, sometime between 1880 and 1885. He said that the officer in command became fast friends with his parents and that they corresponded for many years. He remembered the officer as being Gen. Nelson A. Miles.

T. D. Hunt of rural Attica told a similar story.

Lawrence Maddox told of his father, Walter L. Maddox, who came to Crisfield in 1883, selling beef to the encampment. He was but a small child but he remembered being interested in the horses eating from feed bags. He described the encampment as being a tent city.

The following is a portion of a letter from Mr. Fred T. Wilson of Denver, who is now 95 years old. He writes from personal memory.

"The reason the U.S. soldiers were encamped there (Crisfield) was that there were threatened Indian raids from the Territory. At least I have recollection of such information. Crisfield was about twelve to fourteen miles from the Indian Territory border. It was the brief terminal of the Pan Handle branch of the A. T. and S. F. Railway, then being built to Albuquerque, N. M.

"There were between 1,500 and 2,000 soldiers encamped. The infantry site was just east of town and the cavalry on the west. One of the infantry soldiers died while there and was buried just south of town. A high red-rock wall was built around the grave. The name of 'Waddell' was inscribed on the headstone.

"The soldiers were there some three months and I believe their commander was Gen. Nelson A. Miles."

The legal description of the site is northeast one-fourth of section 20, township 33, range 9 west.

We visited the site and found a number of square cut out portions, with the fourth side open, in the low shale banks for a distance of some two miles. In one we found parts of an old abandoned cook-stove and an ax which had nearly rusted away. We assumed that these cut-outs may have served as field kitchens. There was no evidence of any permanent installation.

Harper County may well have been a corridor for the military and freighters between Fort Leavenworth and Camp Supply in the Territory. The Crisfield camp site may have been visited many times. No civilians lived in the area before 1878 at the earliest so no one was there to note the traffic of the military or freighters.

The following are excerpts from authoritative documents written about events that would have affected the county.
From the book "The Cherokee Strip"
by George Rainey.

"Custer, commanding the Seventh United States Cavalry regiment, had marched from Fort Dodge. A terrific storm prevailed about the time of the arrival of the forces, making it most inconvenient for both men and horses.

"Governor William Crawford of Kansas had resigned his office and had gotten together the Nineteenth Kansas regiment for the purpose of aiding Custer in his southern campaign. This regiment was assembled at Topeka where, just before its departure, a great celebration was had and amidst the waving of good-byes and the blare of bands, the march southward was begun.

"The route lay by way of Camp Crawford, now Wichita, whence the regiment resumed its course to Camp Supply. Encountering the storm and being without tents or other protection, men and horses suffered greatly. Amidst the blinding snow storm the men became bewildered, and lost among the sand hills along the north side of the Cimarron, with rations for men and provender for horses exhausted, their situation was hazardous. Some of the horses were frozen to death and many of the men were so frostbitten that they were practically helpless. At last, on the 28th of November, (1868), they managed to find Custer, with his regiment."

From "Personal Recollections of General
Nelson A. Miles," published in 1896
by The Werner Company, Chicago and New York.

"The situation in respect to Indian affairs grew steadily worse until another formidable expedition commanded by General Hancock was in 1868, sent against the Indians. This expedition traversed the plains country of Kansas and the northern part of Indian Territory, without, however being able to bring the savages to a general engagement."
From page 151. "The Indians remained practically masters of the plains country up to 1874."
From the "Kansas Historical Collections,"
Vol. X, 1907-8

The Nineteenth Kansas Volunteers.
(Interview with Samuel J. Crawford, June 19, 1908)

"After the attack on the Solomon, August 12 to 13, 1868, I telegraphed President Andrew Johnson the details of the depredations committed in that raid, the number of people killed and captured, and tendered him a regiment of volunteers to assist in the protection of the border settlements. In October, General Sherman was authorized to call for a regiment of cavalry, which was speedily organized and equipped for a winter campaign.

"On the 5th of November the regiment, 1200 strong, marched from Topeka to join General Sheridan at Camp Supply, in the Indian Territory. We crossed the Arkansas on the 14th of November, and after a march of 150 miles through rough, unknown country, through what is now the counties of Sedgwick, Sumner,

Harper and Barber in Kansas and Woodward, Oklahoma, with snows from six to twelve inches deep, the advance reached Camp Supply on the 28th. Here I found Generals Sheridan and Custer with the Seventh Cavalry awaiting our arrival. On the march from Wichita to Camp Supply I subsisted the command on buffalo meat, which we obtained on the march in abundance."

*   *   *   *

Wichita, Kansas
July 11, 1908

"George W. Martin, Secretary, Topeka, Kansas:

Dear Sir: I have received the advance sheets of the 'Nineteenth cavalry' by J. A. Hadley, and an extract from the diary of Luther Thrasher. I find that they disagree as to dates. Both agree, however, as does Col. Horace L. Moore, that they left Topeka on November 5, and arrived at the mouth of the Little Arkansas on November 12, 1886. From these and my intimate knowledge of the route, my teams traveling the route constantly, I can follow their march from Topeka to Camp Supply very closely and locate their camping places.

"Our trail ran west from Wichita to Cowskin Grove, seven miles. The Caddoes were camped there, and 'Dutch Bill' was trading with them—had a cabin and a squaw. The command camped there for the first night after leaving Camp Beecher, probably getting a late start. From there they followed the trail to 'Nee-ne-skaw' (Ninnescah) just below the junction—a plain trail. . . . Thence to the Chikaskia there was a plain trail, twenty-five miles, one day's march. Here, of course, they camped; no timber. From there on the trail was scattering, indistinct; known only to ourselves. They camped next on a branch of the headwaters of Bluff Creek. From that on they were lost, traveling at random. They camped on the Medicine Lodge (river), several miles above its mouth. Their proper route was at the junction of Medicine and Salt Fork, where there is an abundance of timber, thence southwest to Eagle Chief, where there is plenty of timber. Instead they reached the Salt Fork some miles above the junction, where there was no timber and a difficult crossing. From there on they were struck by a blizzard which nearly completed their destruction. A competent guide could have avoided most of their woes. . . .

"In the winter of 1867-68 the writer personally made three

trips with loaded teams—a small train—from Towanda to the North Fork of the Canadian, below where Camp Supply was afterwards built; was caught in a blizzard, was captured by a war party of 100 Cheyennes, but always returned safe and sound without loss of a man or animal, or suffering any hardship; we could have taken the Nineteenth Cavalry through just as easily."

James R. Mead

The authors would like to note here that this is the same James R. Mead who helped Jesse Chisholm start down the famous Chisholm Trail with the first load of freight.
From "Personal Recollections of General Nathan A. Miles"
Chapter XXXIV

"In this chapter it will be necessary to revert to occurrences following the transfer from the command of the Department of the Columbia to that of Missouri, and thence to Arizona.

"In 1885, and for some time previous to that year there had been clashing between the interests of the Indians in the Indian Territory and the owners of the immense herds of cattle that roamed over their reservations. This, in the summer of 1885, seemed ready to ripen into open hostilities. A large part of the Territory had been leased, under authority of the government, fenced in, and to some extent stocked with cattle.

On account of this authorized occupation of the Territory by white men connected with the cattle interest, a large number were either permanently located there or moving back and forth through the country to attend to their affairs. It also gave opportunity for a large number of lawless men to travel about the Territory. As a result many disorderly acts were committed against the persons and property of the Indians. This created a feeling of discontent, disaffection and hostility on the part of the Indians toward the white people.

As a result of these disturbances, in July, 1885, I was assigned by the President of the command of the Department of the Missouri, of which department the Indian Territory formed a part, and one-fourth of the army was placed at my disposal. Under telegraphic orders I proceeded from Vancouver, Washington, to General Sheridan's headquarters, Chicago, and thence to the Indian Territory.

Upon investigation I found that, as usual, the Indians were not entirely in the wrong. The disaffected Utes in northern New

Mexico and Colorado were in a most desperate state, and only withheld from actual outbreak by the presence of troops in their midst. Six of their number had been murdered by lawless white men; their reservations had been overrun and their game destroyed. They were nearly starving, their daily ration having been reduced to one-half pound of beef and one-quarter of a pound of flour for each Indian. Happily this last cause of discontent was remedied by the prompt action of Secretary of the Interior, who increased the food allowance. The hostile Apaches were at the same time threatening the frontier of southern New Mexico, and it was necessary to keep troops in that part of the country to guard against their incursion. *The extensive settlements in southern Kansas made it necessary for a large body of troops to remain in the vicinity for their protection.* Bad as was the state of affairs in the Territories adjacent to the Indian Territory, the conditions there threatened immediate and serious hostility between the Indian tribes and the white people living in that Territory and in the states of Texas, Kansas and Colorado. In the company of Lieutenant-General Sheridan I visited the Cheyenne and Arapahoe reservations and found them in a most desperate condition. The Indians were huddled together in disagreeable camps, and were entirely beyond the control of the agent and his Indian police. Two of their prominent men had been murdered, and they were turbulent, disaffected, and on the verge of open hostilities.

"While Lieutenant-General Sheridan listened to complaints, I devoted my attention to the condition of the troops and their proper equipment, organization and supplies, and everything that was required to put them in proper condition for active campaigning in case the United States troops were required.

"The threatening condition soon changed. The President revoked the cattle leases, and the Indians were soon brought under control. A very efficient officer, Captain Lee, was placed in charge of the agency. The reservation was summarily cleared of the lawless white men who infested it and peace and confidence were once more restored. The military garrisons were increased, and affairs speedily became quiet, that the large bodies of troops which had been necessary to call from other departments were returned to their proper stations."

We feel that we have shown proof that the military did pass through Harper County.

If anyone can judge from the letters of those who saw the Crisfield encampment, those who knew General Miles and from the General's writings, one is tempted to place General Nelson A. Miles and his command at the Crisfield encampment.

COUNTY EDUCATION

Rapid Strides in County Education

From "The *Anthony Republican* and *Bulletin*,"
May 20, 1948

"The educational history of the county begins with the year 1879, the first report of a county superintendent of public instruction made July 1, 1879. At that time there were twenty-four school districts, a school population of 683, an enrollment of 214 and an average daily attendance of 141. There was only one schoolhouse in the county, and the valuation of the school property was given as $100.00.

"According to Supt. of Public Instruction, John T. Smith, there are now 36 organized school districts in Harper County with 29 districts operating. There are 45 elementary teachers in the county not including Harper and Anthony schools, which are not under county superintendent supervision, and a total of 60 teachers in the county under county supervision which includes rural high school teachers. Total enrollment in Harper County schools is 585 pupils.

"The total valuation of the Harper County school districts was $34,383,904.00."

Unified School District 361

House Bill No. 377 passed by the 1963 legislature became a law May 15, 1963. It prescribes the procedures to be followed in the organization of unified school districts.

After careful planning all of Harper County, except the area served by the Attica school became Unified District No. 361.

On May 8, 1968, a bond issue for $2,250,000.00 was passed by a vote of 1,377 to 1,051 to build a new Unified High School midway between Anthony and Harper.

The Board Members of Unified School District, 361 of Harper County are as follows:

Gerald Fisher, Harper, Kan.
John Heavin, Harper, Kan.
Dick Watt, Harper, Kan.
Mrs. H. L. Galloway, Anthony, Kan.
LaRue Christy, Anthony, Kan.
Herbert Mathes, Harper, Kan.

From the files of the *"Conway Springs Star,"*
June 25, 1898

"At a school meeting in a neighboring town the question of teachers' wages was being discussed and one of the orators said: Now you can buy a cow for $16.00, but you can get a better one for $20.00; and you can hire a schoolteacher for $15.00 a month but it pays better to pay $20.00 for a good one. Your cheap cow won't give much milk, and it is the same with a cheap schoolteacher."

ART IN HARPER COUNTY

Harper County is steadily becoming the art center of the southwest. The community of Attica was first to start the movement. In 1952 Lola Asper was responsible for the first faltering steps insisting that the study of art would give creative satisfaction and be great fun.

Mrs. G. Wickham of Harper taught a series of ten lessons and the fruits of these early labors were shown at the County Fair where Pat Rowley of Wichita was judge. Mr. Rowley took the Attica group under his wing and taught classes whose ages ranged from 17 to 75 years.

The first exhibit of the class was in the Wichita Art Assn. Gallery in Wichita, in 1953. As a result of this happy experience, the Attica Artist's Guild was formed.

In 1958 the city permitted the jail to be used as a gallery for an art exhibit.

In 1955 *Life* magazine photographers became interested in the activities of the Attica Artists. Six pages in *Life* magazine, August 22, 1955 issue, told their story.

As a result of this outstanding publicity the Attica Artists' Guild was on its way. Invitations to visit interesting places and to exhibit work came from all over the Midwest.

The Artists' Guild was featured in 'Ford Times' in 1956.

The grand opening of the multimillion-dollar Spivey Gasoline Plant north of Attica was a great affair for Attica. On May 4, 1957, Governor Geo. Docking, Senator Andrew Schoepel and J. L. Latimore, president of the Magnolia Petroleum Company (now Mobile) and other dignitaries conducted the ceremonies. Attica artists displayed about 35 paintings of the plant towers, compressors, and gathering system at the Grand Opening. Three of these paintings were purchased and now hang in the offices of the Mobile officials.

In 1957 the Guild purchased "Nine Cottonwood Valley School" built in 1898. The Guild president, Mr. Ray Williamson, had started his teaching career at this school in 1903. Mr. Williamson donated a plot on North Logan Street in Attica. The old schoolhouse was moved to this site. The building was completely remodeled adding a wood-burning fireplace, kitchen and rest room.

Today paintings by Attica artists hang in banks, schools, hospitals, business offices and in many homes.

Art in Harper (City)

Harper enthusiasm began to take on life in the 50's. Mrs. Georgia Wickham taught the earliest art classes, some of her religious paintings now hang in the Presbyterian Church in Harper.

In 1954 a class of six was taught by Helen Ready.

Ellen Clark Crawford, a native Harper Countian, now a New York commercial artist, began to whip the group into professional stature. Mrs. Crawford taught the first children's art classes in Harper.

Through the years the group painted in different downtown buildings, basements and back yards.

The Harper Art Association was organized May 27, 1961 with the following officers: Dorothy Scarlett, Pres.; Carol Long, V. Pres.; Agnes Nye, Sec. and Treas. Etta Le Ford and Robert Branon of Argonia along with the officers comprised the Board of Directors.

A permanent "Downtown Gallery" is located at 105 West Main Street.

In 1962 the Milton, Kansas, Santa Fe Depot was purchased by L. D. Banta, local banker for the association, and was moved to its new foundation near the Harper Historical Museum on East 12th. It houses the permanent collection of the Art Association.

The Harper Association was incorporated in 1965. That year they undertook the Summer Recreation Program teaching some 100 children art and related crafts. This project has become permanent.

The Department of Continuing Education of Kansas State University began holding art courses in the Downtown Gallery in September, 1961 and students from near and far participated. Instructors have been: Prof. Michael Williamson, Manhattan; Don Filby, Wichita; Bob Scott, Kingman. Others who have taught at the Gallery are Betty Dickerson, Jim Davis and Eugene Harwick.

The big event of the year is the Sidewalk Art Festival held the second Saturday in May which was started in 1965. This event is co-sponsored by the Chamber of Commerce, The First National Bank and the Art Association.

The Art Gallery has hosted many one-man shows, among them being, L. Murray, Dorothy Scarlett, G. Wickham, Don Filby, Jim Davis, and a weaving show at the Art Depot by Rosalea of New York City.

Honorary members of the Harper Art Association, Inc., are Dr. John P. Simoni, Betty Dickerson, of Wichita; Jim Davis of Colorado, Eugene Harwick of Hays State College; Ellen Clark Crawford of New York City; Robert Bolitho, Emporia; and Georgia Wickham. Past presidents are Agnes Nye, Carol Long, Fern Crow, and Dorothy Scarlett. Rose Jacobs is the 1968 president.

The first School Museum Art Conference in Kansas was held in the Downtown Gallery February 25, 1967. This event was sponsored by the Wichita Art Museum Members Foundation, Inc., Unified School Dist. No. 254, Medicine Lodge, and the Harper Art Association, Inc.

PORTRAITS

LORENE SQUIRE

Lorene was born in Wellington, Kansas, in 1908, where her father, Harry E. Squire, was Superintendent of Sumner County schools. The family moved shortly thereafter to Madison, Wisconsin, where her father completed his Master's Degree in History at the University of Wisconsin. He subsequently taught history at the University of Wisconsin and Sterling College, Sterling, Kansas. In 1911, he moved to Harper, Kansas, to enter into the furniture business with his father-in-law, L. L. Galloway. Lorene's mother, Lillie M. Squire, had been graduated from Drake University with a degree in Dramatics prior to her marriage, and during her lifetime directed nearly all the stage plays produced in Harper by the high school, the American Legion, and other organizations.

Lorene completed her elementary education in the Harper schools, attended Wichita University and was graduated from Kansas University.

Her photographic work began in earnest at the age of 16 when "Nature Magazine" published some of her bird photographs taken with a Brownie camera.

After she completed her college education, she devoted the rest of her short life to photographing wildfowl and writing about them. Her pictures and articles appeared repeatedly in *Life* and other national magazines here and abroad. Exhibits of her pictures were held in New York and London.

Her book "Wildfowling with a Camera" was published in 1938 by Lippincott. She died on April 12, 1941, at the age of 33 years in an automobile accident in Oklahoma where she had gone to take pictures of prairie chickens.

STELLA AND LEM LAIRD

Harper County may well be proud of a highly intelligent husband and wife.

Lem was born in Parsons, Kansas, September 23, 1884 and has lived over seventy years of his life in Harper County. In 1915 Lem and his sister started the count of nesting and migratory birds. They also banded birds under permit for the U. S. Department of Interior, Fish and Wild Life Service, Laurel, Maryland.

Lem spent several years teaching. It would have been a privilege indeed to have studied under a teacher such as Lem who was dedicated to nature. His students were encouraged to learn about the world in which they lived. The day the first automobile came chugging past his schoolroom all classes were hurriedly dismissed so that all might witness the great new invention. Lem taught Burke, Runnymede, Banner, Grove and Pleasant Valley schools. His teaching certificate was the highest granted at that time.

Miss Stella Morse was born near Tonkawa on a homestead claimed at the opening of the Cherokee Outlet. Having graduated from high school and attending Wichita business college she started her career as a newspaper woman. She was employed for eight years by the Cherokee Publishing Company, Cherokee Oklahoma. On April 17, 1927, Stella Morse and Lem Laird were married.

Now that Lem was a family man he became a farmer and dairyman. Loving nature as he did he studied how his wild animal friends could better the lot of mankind. For many years Lem and his wife and two daughters, Helen and Francis, caught and sold, with permit, live animals and reptiles common to Harper County, to all parts of the world. The Philadelphia Zoo being one of his best clients. Lem's account of catching kangaroo rats along the Chikaskia River is most interesting.

The Laird family set out to make their prairie home a forest home. Thirty-five varieties of trees grow on their farm. A few years ago Lem was given a "Tree Award." An excerpt from the letter telling him of the award reads as follows: "You are now a part of the greatest private conservation movement in America, 31,000 forest landowners have nearly 71 million acres of forest land under good management."

The study of geology held fascination for Lem who is well-versed in some phases, particularly rocks and rock formations. He has collected and polished many rocks found in Harper County. He gave us our first Crisfield Diamond. Among his rocks are petrified wood, quartz, flint, agate, jasper, and quartzite.

Through the years the Lairds have collected many valuable antiques.

One of the yearly chores of these good people is to furnish Christmas trees from their tree farm for some of their close friends.

The Lairds live much as their parents did. Their house is built from cottonwood lumber grown on their property. They depend on wood for fuel to cook their food and warm their home.

Stella and Lem Laird are two of the precious gems to be found in Harper County.

Snake Farming the Unique Industry of L. W. Laird, Harpfr County Farmer

Ships Reptiles to Many Different Countries—Frequently as Many as 1,000 Snakes in His Silo.
Harper, Kansas, August 30 (Special)

This county has one very busy farmer, L. W. Laird, living four and a half miles north of Harper, who includes in his diversified farming and stock raising, a thrifty business of snake-raising, collecting and marketing, which nets him a neat monthly income. This is rather the best season of the year for shipment and he makes tri-weekly and sometimes daily consignments.

This week Mr. Laird packed a large box for a thirty-day shipment to France by way of the Hagenbeck Company, located at Hoboken, N. J., which is the largest institution of its kind in the United States. It is estimated that one bull snake, two and one-half feet long, will eat 150 mice and rats annually and since these rodents are largely responsible for the spread of plagues, snakes are a great assistance in exterminating after-war pests and plagues. Bull snakes at $1.00 each are a cheap investment and an asset to any farm.

Laird not only raises snakes but has established quite an industry of snake catching among the small boys. His silo is used for their home and frequently contains a thousand. Evening is the best time to see them.

The assortment at this time is confined to blue racers, spreading vipers, bull snakes, water moccasins and garter snakes. His stock of rattlers has been exhausted but he leaves soon for New Mexico to replenish with rattlers, horned toads and other reptiles peculiar to that climate. A recent shipment to Bourbonville, Kentucky, included a number of prairie dogs.

The rattlers command the best price because of the various uses to which their hides can be turned.

(We do not know the year of this clipping.)

C. C. ZOLLARS

C. C. Zollars of Harper, Kansas, was born in Martin County, north of Lincolnville, Indiana, in 1890.

Mr. Zollars' father died at an early age leaving the wife and several sons. After a time the mother brought her children to Kansas.

Upon arriving in Kansas he performed the usual tasks that were available to youngsters, worked in the broomcorn and did ranch work. He completed high school and attended Kansas State, at Manhattan, majoring in education and studying music. He later attended Central Business College in Kansas City where he worked on the "*Kansas City Star.*"

Moving to Harper County he took up farming. On October 29, 1914 he was united in marriage to Clara Knoche. Mr. Zollars says that she was the prettiest girl that he had ever seen. The Zollars have a family of four children, all of whom are college graduates.

C. C. received a government citation for his ability to sell government bonds during World War II.

The Danville elevator was organized with the help of Mr. Zollars.

At one time he was candidate for the State Senate. He served eleven years on the Harper High School Board, some time on the advisory board of Phillips University, Enid, Oklahoma. Has been active in the music and has served as elder in the Harper Christian Church for many years. Mr. Zollars is past president of 'War Dads,' chapter No. 46. At present he is president of the Harper Historical Society and has been president for a number of years.

Mr. C. C. Zollars was invited to be listed in Marquis' "WHO'S WHO, Inc." in 1965.

The Zollars have four children: Leland H., Millard C., Arlene Zollars Woods, and Norma Zollars Henderson.

Mrs. Zollars passed away, Aug. 6, 1968.

DR. H. L. GALLOWAY

"The *Wichita Eagle*,"
Jan. 16, 1966

ANTHONY'S 'DOC' IS STRONG AT 80

by Forest Hintz

Anthony, Kansas — Dr. H. L. Galloway is beginning to question some of the things he learned in medical school.

"They told us we'd have to quit at 45," he said. "They claimed we'd be too old to practice beyond that age."

"Doc," as he is affectionately known by everyone in Harper County, still is going strong at 80. He has no intention of quitting, nor does anyone want him to.

"They also told us we'd grow to hate the practice of medecine," he continued. "I've loved every minute of it. True, medecine is a jealous mistress and a doctor never stops studying, but I've never regretted it."

Dr. Galloway was born and reared in Harper County. He had two years of college at Emporia before enrolling in the Drake University Medical School at Des Moines, Iowa. He served his internship in Mercy Hospital there as night police surgeon, complete with horse-drawn ambulance. He returned to Anthony in 1911.

"The first couple of years were rough," he said. "My income the first year was $750. There were 21 doctors in the county then and today there are only six. It was hard for a young man to get started."

But he got started and became known as one of the finest surgeons in Kansas.

"We had no real hospitals then," he recalled. "There wasn't any ambulance service, so you went to the patient. You got a nurse to help you and did most of the surgery on the kitchen table.

"Laboratories were another thing we didn't have then. A doctor had to know what was wrong with the patient; he could not guess or wait for the lab reports. He had to make his diagnosis and decide what to do right then, and he had to be right.

"The flu epidemic hit us in 1918, and it was a bad one. Sometimes I'd see 100 patients a day, perform five or six operations and that night drive miles making the rounds. It was hard work but I loved every minute of it.

"Some of the things that happened then would make us shudder today," Dr. Galloway continued. "I remember performing an operation for another doctor in a neighboring town. He gave the anesthetic and was to help with the operation, but in the middle he had to answer the front door. Then he went down to the basement and stoked the furnace before he came back."

Dr. Galloway estimated that he performed "several thousand" operations and delivered an average of 200 babies each year. "I don't really know," he said. "I've often wished I'd kept a diary, but never had the time.

"Finally I opened a little hospital on the second floor of a building on Main Street, (Anthony) and used it for 30 years. We didn't have an elevator; we just carried the patients upstairs and hoped they would be able to walk down."

In 1941 the city of Hardtner built a hospital with the funds donated in the will of Jacob Achenbach, early day financier. The will provided that Dr. Galloway be responsible for the hospital, and for 20 years he drove 40 miles to Hardtner every other day. Hanging on his office wall is a plaque presented to him in 1961 by the citizens of Hardtner.

But "Doc" did manage to take a vacation nearly every year. He would allow himself two weeks—observing surgery at the Mayo Clinic at Rochester, Minn. "A doctor has to keep up with the advances," he explained.

"People are living longer now but I don't think they are any healthier," he said.

"I think a doctor should become friends with his patients and get to know them." As he spoke a woman brought in a loaf of still-warm bread. "I baked it this morning," she said. "I made an extra loaf for you."

"That's what I mean," Dr. Galloway said. "These people are my friends."

His statement was borne out by random comment downtown. One man summed up the general feeling with, "If Doc came downtown and said we all had leprosy we'd know we all had leprosy, even if we didn't know what it was. Somehow, he just seems to know.

"You can't say he's a part of Anthony. He is Anthony."

*   *   *   *

Dr Galloway is now associated with the Anthony Hospital. On March 11, 1968, Dr. H. L. Galloway was named Honorary Chief of Staff for life.

AGNES AND BILL NYE

Agnes Louise Nye was born June 22, 1919 to Iva G. and H. F. Stalder in Meade, Kansas. The Stalder family came to Harper in 1933 where Agnes attended public schools. After high school graduation she was employed with the First National Bank in Harper as clerk and secretary until 1951.

Agnes and Warren William (Bill) Nye were married in 1945. They have lived all their married life in Harper.

Painting and historical research became hobbies early in Agnes' life, later her art became her career. She receives her degree in her chosen field from Wichita State University in 1969. Mrs. Nye will help organize the art department in the new unified school district which covers nearly all of Harper County.

Extensive research and study on the Runnymede Colony is one of her pet projects. Her oils hang in nearly every state.

No one could be a better "Chamber of Commerce" booster than Mrs. Nye. Through her dedicated spirit and tactful grace she has helped boost many worthwhile projects for the town that she loves.

When asking someone in Harper County, "Do you know Agnes Nye?" the person being questioned usually gets that 'misty look' and answers, "Oh yes, she is my best friend."

Many honors have come her way: "Who's Who of American Women," 1968-69, fifth edition, 1969-70, sixth edition, commended for civic leadership, historical research and art. She is also listed in Who's Who in the Midwest" and in "Dictionary of International Biography," fifth edition, 1968-69, London, England.

Agnes is a member of Alpha Omega, Chapter of Kappa Pi at Wichita State University, a member of the Museum of Modern Art, in New York City and she belongs to the National League of American Pen Women.

*   *   *   *

Warren William Nye was born May 31, 1918, at Harper, Kansas. He was educated in the public schools of the county.

While serving in World War II in the army, he was wounded at St. Lo, France in combat. He received the Combat Infantry Badge, Purple Heart, and Combat Battle Star for the Normandy landing. Bill was Staff Sergeant, C Co. 320 Inf. Div. Following the Normandy landing he was hospitalized for thirteen months.

Bill was the Harper postmaster from August 1, 1946 to October 17, 1959, at which time he chose to assume the duties of rural mail carrier.

Bill is an artist in the field of sculpture, winning awards for his outstanding work.   Golf is his sport and he has won several trophies in competition.

Both Agnes and Bill are active in the Harper United Methodist Church.

A Country Gentleman, Hardy Herst

He walks erectly in the April sunshine with screaming peacocks at his heels. The warm west wind brings remembrances. His favorite Morgan gives him an affectionate nuzzle as he passes by.

Hardy Herst was born in 1883 in this prairie land. His parents, Mellisa and David, homesteaded east of the present town of Freeport, near Argonia, Kansas. There were seven children in the family. His young years were steeped in tales of wagon trains and pioneer adventures. He witnessed the hanging of a cattle rustler near his home.

In another April in the faraway 80's Hardy went with his family to the Baptist Church services in Argonia and as was the pioneer custom, at the close of services all the families gathered at one homestead. Before the dinner bell sounded it was discovered that one of the children was missing. It was little Pete, a neighbor's child. All the men left the prospects of their Sunday dinner and began to search the banks of the nearby stream, the barn and shed and last year's tall dry grass that could hide a small boy.

The day wore on and little Pete's mother went to her home to wait. After hours of searching the men returned shaking their heads, "No little Pete."

The distraught mother, forgetting her grief for a time said,

"You must all be tired and hungry, I haven't much to cook but I have flour to make a big pan of biscuits. Rest a spell and I'll get busy."

So the mother went to the flour barrel—there was little Pete —asleep in the flour.

In 1893, the year of the opening of the Cherokee Outlet, Hardy was ten years old. Some of his family were going to make the run for land. Hardy had managed a ride as far as the state line and starting point. He perched himself in a tree in Ryle King's yard.

Soldiers, to give the starting signal, had been stationed at one-half mile intervals along the starting line. At a given signal the first shot was fired at the eastern end to be answered by the next soldier to the west until the signal was heard along the Kansas border.

At the gun-shot signal a vast cloud of dust rose. The noise and confusion were beyond belief. Hardy had witnessed and would always remember this historic happening.

Hardy attended public schools, later he ventured into the world of higher learning at Emporia State. He made his own way at various jobs, hack driving and keeping the dormitory dining room filled with paying guests.

Once when returning home by way of Herington, Kansas, Hardy stopped to change trains. Some local football players greeted him and asked him to stay and help them in a football game against a neighboring team. Hardy had played some football for Emporia State, so he consented.

As Hardy told the story years later, "I could see one foot coming for me and another—I never took such a beating—the next morning I thought I would die standing up. I vowed that I would never go on a football field again, and I never did."

Some time later Hardy went to the West coast where he visited San Francisco before the great earthquake; then on to Los Angeles where he worked as a streetcar conductor. Many happy memories were gathered there, and he returned to Freeport with a moneybelt filled with gold pieces.

Hardy, being interested in agriculture, exchanged his gold for mules and farm equipment.

A great love for collecting and preserving memorabilia developed in the personality of Hardy Herst. All his adult life he has been classed as a collector of stature. His desire to be well-groomed became manifest. He always dressed as the "Country Gentleman" complete with necktie.

After establishing a home near Freeport he married Cora Mummy and became the father of two children, David and Mary Virginia. These were the years of fulfillment. He bred and raised registered Morgan horses, collected thousands of beautiful and unique pieces ranging from rare books to patterned glass. His wife Cora, died and he found happiness again in marriage. His second marriage was to Edith Barrett Springer.

Hardy became known wherever Morgan horses were raised. He judged many horse shows and was considered an authority on horses.

Perhaps no home in southern Kansas has had more callers than that of Hardy Herst. Many came to sup of his cup of friendly philosophy, others to study his fabulous collections.

Hardy's son David lives in Arkansas and his daughter, Mary Virginia Tompkinson lives near by. She teaches in the Harper schools. Her life's story is full of adventure: mission work in Asia, rescue by the *Gripsholm* during the Second World War, military service, and years of teaching.

May many Aprils smile upon you, as the peacocks scream and your favorite horse looks on, Country Gentleman.

RAYMOND L. HAYTER

From notes by Mr. Hayter

Raymond L. Hayter, son of Nannie E. and Hill C. Hayter, was born near Possum Trot, Green County, Missouri, on January 16, 1879.

As an infant he came with his parents and brother in a covered wagon, to a 160-acre farm seven miles southwest of Anthony. The farm had been purchased a year earlier. The family lived in the covered wagon until a two-room house could be built. The family sold their farm and went to Commanche County, ten miles northwest of Coldwater to prove up a claim. They lived in a half sod, half dugout dwelling.

The route from Coldwater by way of Medicine Lodge to Anthony was extremely difficult to travel. There was only a trail, no fences, the only tree to be seen was one north of the present Anthony airport. In Anthony there were no modern conveniences. There was a town well located in the center of the street between the Citizens National Bank and the Limbard Hill building. The well was operated by a rope and pully and two wooden buckets. Anthony was indeed a pioneer town at that time.

Our family returned to Harper County and bought a 160-acre farm near our first farm. This was the home where we were to grow up, my brothers, Clarence, now deceased, Floyd and I. A little sister was born here but she failed to live.

Fuel was a problem in those days, we burned mostly cow and buffalo chips. Neighbors went together into the 'Strip' to the Salt Fork to get wood to burn.

I was a member of the first brass band organized in the county, the date was about 1890. The band was known as the Empire Township Brass Band.

My first real estate was the purchase of a farm in the southwest part of the county. I was able to make the purchase through the kindness and trust of A. B. Small. There were no improvements on my land so I bought myself a tent from an Orient railroad gang who were breaking camp. They sold me the tent and threw in a bulldog who became my friend and companion. I pitched my 'rag house' on my farm and became known in the Corwin and Hazelton communities as the 'Rag man'. I often received mail addressed to "The Rag Man."

In 1904 I was married to Mamie M. Miller. We built a house and barn and started our life together. We became active members of the Corwin Presbyterian Church. After moving to Anthony, some time later, we moved our membership to the First Congregational Church in Anthony.

In 1904, I helped organize the First State Bank of Corwin, and was a charter member of the Board of Directors. In 1908 I became president and remained so until 1944 when the bank was sold to the Hazelton State Bank.

In 1915, my brother Floyd and I bought an interest in a hardware store which had been established in 1883. We were in this business for several years.

I am a great lover of horses and mules. I owned the largest mule I ever saw, he weighed 1,960 pounds. All events concerning horses were of interest to me. I was president of the Anthony Saddle Club and chairman of the Fair Board for some time.

There were two sons born to us, C. Dwight, who is in the farm management business in Anthony and Lloyd L., farmer and stockman who lives near Anthony.

THE MUIRS

Probably no family has been more colorful or has been held in higher esteem than the Muir family.

Their story goes back many years to young W. G. Muir who chose medicine as a profession. He graduated from the University of Michigan by hard work. He would teach school for a time, then return to the university where he would stoke furnaces to help his finances.

In 1884 Dr. Muir came to Harper where he set up an office and began the practice of medicine. A young woman, Miss Lizzie Palin, came to his office suffering from an infected finger. Perhaps it was love at first sight as they were married a short time later.

Dr. Muir learned to manipulate finances in his struggles at the university. Payment in money was difficult to get from his patients so he devised a plan. He asked those who owed him to make the payment of their bills in corn (which was plentiful that year). He credited each bushel ten cents above market price. Great open cribs were made and filled. Dr. Muir realized a handsome return.

Dr. Muir was elected Mayor of Harper in 1893, '95, '97, 1903, 1907, and resigned March 9, 1908 and was elected mayor again in 1911 and 1913. The Muirs had one son, Donald Palin Muir. Donald Muir was educated in the public schools of Harper County and attended the University of Kansas where he earned a law degree. There he met his future wife, Blanche N. Barko.

Blanche Barko was born at Mulberry, Kansas. Her father died as the result of a farm accident. The mother took her small children to Lawrence, Kansas, where she obtained a large house, using the two top floors as a fraternity house for law students.

Blanche graduated in 1911 from K.U. with a degree in public school music and soon earned a master's degree in organ. She had made her way teaching in the school, grading papers, and tutoring German, French, and Italian.

After the marriage of Donald and Blanche, they made their home in Anthony, Kansas, where they established a law firm. Donald Muir became active in politics holding various offices including two terms in the State Legislature.

One son, W. G., named for grandfather Muir, was born to the Donald Muirs in 1914.

Mrs. Donald Muir became active in many fields. She served a four-year appointment on the Kansas Crippled Children's Commission, worked unstintingly for the Federation of Women's Clubs, worked for the betterment of the blind, founded the Kansas Branch of the Women's Field Army (Cancer), served one term as a member of the Kansas Board of Regents and assisted Mr. Muir in his political career.

She died in 1962 after years of invalidism.

W. G. Muir attended Wichita University, Kansas University Law School and was graduated from Washburn Law School with a degree in law in 1937. He served in World War II. W. G. Muir is an accomplished musician, performing for a time with the noted composer, T. Lieurance. He has knowledge and skill in the field of electronics.

Harper claimed him as their city attorney for 15 years. In 1949 he joined his father's law firm in Anthony which is still maintained.

W. G. Muir and Martina Clarkson were married in 1960. Martina Muir has a pioneer background of interest. She is the granddaughter of Dr. H. Martin who came to Harper among the earlier settlers. Dr. Martin was a man of charm and ability in many fields. One story is told of Dr. Martin which gives one view of his personality. Word had been telegraphed to Harper that the Dalton boys of Coffeyville were on their way to sack the town. The timing was right as the "strip" had been opened only a short time before. With the men gone, Harper was almost defenseless. John Baumstark opened his hardware and provided a small arsenal and Dr. Martin climbed to the roof of the tallest building and set up his telescope. Dr. Martin enjoyed the reputation of being an excellent shot; naturally he was the one to take the roof-top position. Some were surprised to see him kneeling as if in prayer. Some said that he was praying for the protection of Harper; others said that he was praying that the Daltons would show as there was a handsome price on their heads!

The W. G. Muirs live in Harper.

HARPER COUNTY LOOKS TO ITS YOUTH

Carol Drouhard Long and her husband, W. C. (Corky) Long, Jr., should be numbered among Harper County's strong young people who are going places. They are the parents of five children. Carol is active outside her home, developing into an artist of note and taking part in civic affairs. Before marriage she taught in the Conway Springs public school system.

Mr. Long is a state representative from Harper County.

*   *   *   *

Rankin L. Greisinger, son of Mr. and Mrs. A. L. Greisinger of Anthony, holds a B.A. degree in journalism from Wichita State University and has done graduate work at the University of the Philippines in Manilla.

From 1951 to '58, Mr. Greisinger was with the United States Air Force with the rank of captain, served as Information Officer at Wing, Division and Air Force level. During the final two years of service was Aide de Camp to Commander Air Material Command, Pacific. He resigned U.S.A.F. in 1958 to join the Cessna Aircraft Co.

At present Mr. Greisinger is Sales Promotion Manager, Commercial Aircraft Division for Cessna.

His wife is the former Kay Clarahan. They have five daughters and reside in Wichita, Kansas.

*   *   *   *

Dr. Jess Charles, Jr., grew up in Attica, Kansas, and was graduated from the Attica High School in 1946. After a tour of duty with the United States Army, he entered Kansas University where he received his B.S. degree in 1952. In 1956 he received an M.D. degree from the Kansas University School of Medicine. He did his internship at Valhalla, New York. Then he received the residency doctorship at Rockland State Hospital.

Dr. Charles is a psychiatrist. He has a private practice in Ridgewood, New Jersey and also works at Berger Pines Hospital.

* * * *

Carolyn Kay Joyner of Freeport, Kansas, an unusually beautiful young woman, holds many scholastic, civic and beauty awards and commendations. Her record reads as follows:

Miss Anthony, 1960—Arkalalah Queen
Miss Anthony, 1961—K.N.P.A. Contest, first runner-up
Miss Kakeland, 1961—Miss Kansas Contest, second runner-up
Miss K.N.P.A., 1962, won title
Miss N.P.P.A., 1962, won title
Miss United States, 1962
International Beauty Congress, 1962, won fourth place
Miss Kansas Wheat Queen, 1963-64, won title
Miss Future Business Executive, 1963 (Emporia State)
Miss Joan of Arc, 1963
Miss Navy Wings of Gold, 1964

As a result of these honors Miss Joyner made a world tour. She received her Master of Science degree from Kansas State College, Emporia, Kansas, in 1967.

Miss Joyner has taken up teaching as a profession.

* * * *

Miss Nancy Gates, teen-age daughter of Mr. and Mrs. Dale Gates of rural Anthony, is an outstanding young person having won the National Little Britches Rodeo Championship for the second time, winning in 1963 and again in 1966 at which time she was only 13 years old. Her championship in 1963, when she was but 10 years old crowned her as the youngest champion ever.

In the 1966 event she won seven trophies, an engraved saddle, a pair of Justin boots and three gold and silver belt buckles.

At present Nancy is a sophomore in the Anthony High School. She was runner-up in the Kansas State High School Rodeo (1968).

Rex Gates, brother of Nancy, was National Champion Little Britches performer, boy's division, 1963. He was champion bull dogger, Little Britches Rodeo in 1967. At the high school and college rodeo at Alva, 1968, he was judged as "best all around cowboy."

Rex plans to attend the 1968 semester of college, having completed his high school in Anthony.

Rex and Nancy buy, break and train their own horses.

They are the grandchildren of Mr. and Mrs. Charlie Carothers. Charlie is the man shown servicing a windmill in this volume.

*   *   *   *

Attica has a wonderful record of young people who have entered the medical profession: Jane Montzino Berman, Jack Hillard, Bryce Ballard and Jess Charles, Jr.

TAPESTRY

The most warm hearted and often gifted people make up the skeins of life's tapestry in Harper County. These people of vast rolling prairies, living streams and thousands of planted trees along with rustling majestic native cottonwoods surely are beloved by the Almighty.

The weaving of this tapestry started in 1876 when the first people came to dwell in this land. There are many fascinating stories of their lives. One fine example is the Diary of Theo. B. Marsh. Mary Walton Brown Whittington's life is recorded in the "Whitting-Brown" geneology; it is almost beyond belief. The courage, strength and wisdom of this pioneer woman are astounding. Mary Whittington lived in the Camchester area.

Some of the darker threads are woven from the Treadwell Story. Walter E. Treadwell, a wealthy young man, came from New York to Harper County in the 1880's. He established a ranch of 8,860 acres. Frances Glenn, sister of the Glenn brothers of Harper (city) founding fame, married W. S. Forey of Chicago and Wichita. Francis became the step-mother to Forey's two beautiful daughters by a former marriage.

Eventually the Foreys came to Harper where Treadwell met and married the younger daughter, taking her to live on his ranch.

Before his marriage, Treadwell had taken a partner, Charles Clark, who was young and handsome. Treadwell, who shunned society, allowed his partner to assume the role of escort for his bride.

To make a miserable tale short, Treadwell realized that he had thrown his wife into the arms of his partner and in a fit of jealous rage encountered Clark in the Bennett Hotel in Anthony and shot him. Mrs. Treadwell followed Clark's body to New York but returned to her husband and by her testimony, Treadwell was freed. Treadwell died of cancer.

A story of another famous Harper County rancher is that of H. B. Waldron, who acquired vast land holdings near the present town-site of Waldron.   J. Howard Wilcox gave an account as given by his father to the effect that Waldron appeared to be a bachelor and lived at an Anthony hotel. He made frequent trips to his ranch driving the finest white horses. Wilcox says that Waldron was a "dandy" in regard to dress, choosing the best tailors and affecting lace fluting from his coat cuffs.

Out of the blue a woman appeared calling herself Mrs. Waldron. According to abstracts of his property her name is shown at that time. The story of the struggles of the town of Waldron is told elsewhere in this volume. Waldron eventually left Kansas and spent the rest of his life in France.

There are many fine threads of this tapestry which have lost their identity with the passing of time. These people we salute. They are a part of the weaving but we can no longer separate the threads or color.

The Neff sisters of Harper, Maggie and Dottie, represent the refinement, grace, charm and accomplishments necessary to make Victorian ladies. With their passing, the perfume of their lives remains. Maggie was a public speaker and writer, contributing to the *Topeka Daily Journal, Wichita Eagle* and newspapers of the county. Dottie was a vocalist of distinction.

Judge Myrtle Youngburg retired January 11, 1965 after 48 years of law practice. It was a long road from schoolteacher to self-trained and educated member of the bar.

Myrtle Youngberg was born in 1895 and came to Harper County when she was three years old. She was educated in the common schools of the time. After teaching in country schools for four years she attended Wichita Commercial College. In 1903 she took a position with the law firm of C. E. Wilcox. She studied law and was admitted to the bar in 1916. Miss Youngberg continued to practice law with C. E. Wilcox and later with J. Howard Wilcox in the firm of Wilcox and Wilcox. In 1952 she was elected probate judge of Harper County, a post she held for over twelve years until her retirement.

Threads of lovely colors and strength are those of Iva G. and Herbert F. Stalder of Harper. They have given unstintingly of their time and themselves to make Harper a better community in which to live.

The Fisher family gave several threads to the tapestry. Charles and Electa Woodward Fisher settled near Danville in the 80's. They were prosperous farm people and good parents to their children. Charles' brothers and sisters followed from West Virginia. Joe Fisher taught the second term of school in Odell Township. The schoolroom was under J. W. Cleous' kitchen. Tom Fisher was a veterinarian. Jacob lived in Albion and taught school there. Kate Fisher Smith lived with her husband Mill near Bluff City. William Duffy, County Clerk of Harper County from 1892 to 1896 was married to Emma Fisher. Present-day County Commissioner Ata Fisher is the son of Joe Fisher. Gerald of the Freeport area, son of Ata Fisher, is a board member of Unified District No. 361.

Margaret Hawes Ballard came to Attica from Butler County, Kansas. She was born December 2, 1885. Her husband V. B. Ballard was a druggist in Attica. Mrs. Ballard was active in Federated Women's Club work being state president at one time. She served as an observer for the General Federation of Women's Clubs at United Nations. She was with UNESCO; this work took her abroad.

The Ballards had two children, Dr. Brice Ballard and Francis Ballard Schiff.

Mrs. Ballard died January 17, 1964.

Arthur Clark of Harper adds threads of gold to the tapestry. He was in the milling industry in Harper, Indianapolis and New Orleans during his working years. He tells of his pioneer father who had a claim east of Harper, hitching two teams of mules to a log and pulling the log to Wellington to mark a road between the two places.

In 1895 when Arthur was just a lad, word came to their home that the mother of some of their friends who lived in the "Strip" had passed away. No one but Arthur was at home when the word came so he felt duty bound to go into the Strip and take the sad message. Borrowing a bicycle, he set out. Mr. Clark recalled that the south wind was blowing freely and he became nearly exhausted. Upon reaching the Salt Fork the problem of getting across presented itself, so he sat down to wait until someone else needed to cross. Finally a peddler driving his cart came along and Arthur put his wheel in the cart and he managed a ride.

Night was falling but he kept on what he hoped was the true course. A dim light loomed in the distance. Arthur made for the light and found a young man living on his claim. He spent the night and his host insisted that he borrow his pony to finish his journey.

He reached his friends who immediately started for Harper. After returning the pony to his new friend he placed his bicycle in the Harper-bound wagon. As they neared Manchester the rain started to come down. Arthur decided to go home the rest of the way by train so he left the bicycle in the wagon and went to a Manchester hotel. There he reviewed his finances being the sum of sixty cents. Fifty cents would go for his hotel room, ten cents for a good breakfast but how about the forty-five cents for the train fare home?

He approached the manager of the hotel and asked if there was something that he could do to earn his night's lodging, and if there was would he please let him have his fifty cents back so he could use it for train fare home to Harper. Arthur didn't know there were so many dirty dishes in the world.

Next morning the rain had stopped and he bought his train fare for forty-five cents and arrived in Harper with five cents in his pocket. His family was glad to see him but gave him a sound scolding for leaving home without telling anyone.

Arthur Clark married Mattie Walton, daughter of Louis Walton. Mrs. Clark passed away in 1967. Their daughters are Ellen Clark Crawford, New York City; Martha Clark DeSipio, Washington, D.C.; Elizabeth Clark Stephens, Indianapolis, Ind.; and Louise Clark Hamilton, Rock Island, Ill.

Fern and Merle Crow add color to the tapestry threads. Fern is one of the more talented artists of Harper County and Kansas, having received significant awards. Her work is a joy to behold. Merle (G. M.) is a division manager for a public utility company. A salute to good citizens.

Two strong threads come from present-day Freeport. They are the lives of Hugh and Grace Ransom. Grace is an active member of D.A.R. and Daughters of American Colonists doing research for both organizations. Mr. Ransom is one of the excellent farmers of Harper County.

Brightly colored threads of Harper are those of Dorothy and F. M. Scarlett. Dorothy was not born in Harper County but was born in what was the old Strip. However, Harper has been her adopted home for many years.

The Scarletts deserve much praise for their efforts to place Harper "on the map." Dorothy is a fine artist and gives of her strength and time to the art center. She was the first president of the Harper Art Association. F. M. Scarlett was chairman of the county fair for some time.

The Scarletts maintain an implement business in Harper. They have one daughter, Sandra.

From Freeport again we find good threads for the tapestry. They are Josephine and Bill Greve. Josephine Moyer and William John Greve were married on March 24, 1924 and have maintained a farm home near Freeport since that time. They have two sons, William H. of Freeport and Robert W. who is with the U. S. Department of Agriculture in Oklahoma City.

Josephine is an accomplished needlewoman and genealogist, and a member of the D.A.R.

Many beautiful and special threads are found about whom thousands of words could be written. Among these are Hope and Noah Bauer, whose home is furnished with carefully choosen antiques. Mrs. Bauer is an artist with floral creations.

Charles W. Manninger and his wife Nellie are salt of the earth citizens giving of their time and talents for all they believe to be worthwhile.

Edith McIntire's thread will be of silver to denote her strength of character, stability and temperate nature.

Mr. Roy Carr will have a powerful thread to show that he is a pillar of strength and an ever present help to Harper County.

Before we leave the tapestry of Harper (city) we must note Miss Florence Hudson who has lived with much of the history of the county. When the crowns are laid out for humanity, Miss Florence will find one designed just for her.

One more beautiful thread must be added to round out the color, that of Walter Elbe of Harper who is an artist of exceptional ability using wood as his medium.

Let us say goodby with this simple grace by John McCombe.

> Back of the loaf is the snowy flour,
> And back of the flour is the mill,
> And back of the mill is the wheat and shower,
> And the sun and the Father's will.

HISTORICAL SOCIETY

LIFE MEMBERSHIPS AND DONATIONS GIVEN TO
HARPER CITY HISTORICAL SOCIETY, INC., 1959-1968

Tom S. Hudson
C. C. Zollars
L. D. Banta
Everett L. Mathes
Vera M. Gill
Lloyd E. Mathes
Rev. James Detweiler
Mr. and Mrs. W. A. Tihen
Harper Livestock Sale
Ralph Haskin
Harper Advocate—Bob Bolitho
Brownell-Wiley
Charles V. Maninger
John W. Minger
Farmers Oil Company
Dresser Agency
Mrs. Mary C. Dresser
Harold Bebermeyer
A. E. Smithhisler
C. D. Comer
Southwestern Bell Telephone
    Company
M. W. Renollet
Olin M. Bare
Millard Zollars
Jesse Stucky
Adamson Oil Company
R. H. Watt
Cecil Sharp
Mr. and Mrs. R. E. Bellar
Harper Trucks, Inc.
Beryl Gill
E. F. Campbell
Ralph W. Antrim
Calverts
Ralph W. Springer
Earl Williams

United Gas Service
Hoover Super Service
E. E. Williams
Leo Drouhard
C. A. Bebermeyer
Anthony Farmers Co-op
Western Light and Telephone
    Company
Audra V. George
Roy Boyts
Coffee Shop—Wanda Reida
Hart Floral and Greenhouse
Ben Franklin—Charles Nichols
F. E. Van Valkenburg
Ed Ruhsert
Art Wene
Paul Wohlschlegel
H. F. Stalder
R. and E. Construction
Lena Dryden
John Chevraux
Mrs. Mary E. W. Davis
Mrs. Bertha M. Smith
Mrs. Frances Cunningham
H. Mathes
Mr. and Mrs. John W. Heavin
M. C. Seyb
Thurman Western Auto
George Leeper
W. H. Vornauf
Wm. Lester Hostetler
Charles J. Chandler
Mrs. Claude Braden
Walter Elbe
Charles B. Wolf
Mrs. C. E. Wolf
Mervin Dent

Mrs. Mabel Holland
C. V. Terrell
E. F. Winpigler
Rudy Havlik
Mrs. Lela Snyder
G. D. Rousseau
Roy Pykiet
Hoyt Hoover
John J. Olivier
A. B. Clark
Mattie Clark
Francis Yoder
Oklahoma Tire and Supply
Harper Food Market
Elvin's Store
Ethel Moore
Carl Brown
John Thompson
Mitchell Grocery
I.G.A. Store—John Duffield
Bob Hoover Agency
F. W. Briner
E. W. Miller
Amanda Renollet
Willis Bear
Martin S. Hall
Earl Van Valkenburg
Ollie E. Babcock
Edith G. Litsey
Ben Titus
Dr. K. A. Bush
W. C. Long, Jr.
Frank Palmer
James Compton
Earl Boyts

Martina Clarkson Muir
Mr. and Mrs. Marvin Thiel
Charles Hadsall
B. P. W. Club
H. H. Herst
Mrs. Anna Stuchal
Ed Gerber
Stella Parker
Warren William Nye
Agnes Nye
Salome A. Carius
Marie D. Rapp
Lois D. Hauter
Katheryn D. Beal
Edith McIntire
Ed McGivney
J. W. Daniels
Levi Rymph
Mrs. Samuel Rapp, Jr.
Mrs. Elizabeth Kendall
Henry Washbon
Arnold Warden
Clara Zollars
Jean Zollars
Iva G. Stalder
Joy L. Clements
Carol Long
Gail Bellar
Erma Bea Palmer
Tom Minton
Byron Childs
Mac's Cafe—Coy and Virginia
    McDowell
Edith Fulton

MEMBERS OF HARPER HISTORICAL SOCIETY (active)

Earl McFrederick
C. C. Zollars
Mrs. C. C. Zollars
Edith McIntire
Charles W. Manninger
Nellie E. Manninger
Olin Bare
Earl Boyts
Carl Brown
Noah Bauer
Hope Bauer
W. W. Nye

Agnes Nye
Iva Stalder
H. F. Stalder
Lem Laird
Stella Laird
Mrs. Dorothy Scarlett
Lester Hostetler
George Durant
Florence Durant
Ida Bare
Florence Hudson

ACKNOWLEDGEMENTS

Mary Virginia Tompkinson, Freeport, Kansas
Hardy Herst. Freeport, Kansas
Mr. and Mrs. W. W. Nye, Harper, Kansas
Mr. and Mrs. Wm. Greve, Freeport, Kansas
Lois Barrett, Anthony, Kansas
J. Howard Wilcox, Anthony, Kansas
Mr. and Mrs. Hershal Roach, Anthony, Kansas
Mr. and Mrs. John Smith, Anthony, Kansas
Mr. and Mrs. Kenneth Russell, Duquoin, Kansas
Rev. and Mrs. Earl Buckwalter, Crystal Springs, Kansas
Lillian Hollister Shaw, Canadian, Texas
Mr. Robert Richmond, State Archivist, Kansas State Historical
    Society, Topeka, Kansas
Mr. Thomas Witty, State Archaeologist, Kansas State Historical
    Society, Topeka, Kansas
Charles K. Bayne, Geolgist, United States Department of
    Interior
Geological Survey and State Geological Survey of Kansas, Uni-
    versity of Kansas, Lawrence.
Mrs. Hugh Ransom, Freeport, Kansas
Ida Ellen Rath, Dodge City, Kansas
Mr. and Mrs. James Chism, Anthony, Kansas
Mrs. Alice Henline, Anthony, Kansas
Mr. and Mrs. N. L. Hughbanks, Hutchinson, Kansas
Mr. Tom Fanning, Anthony, Kansas
Mr. and Mrs. A. L. Greisinger, Anthony, Kansas
Mr. and Mrs. Lee Rucker, Medicine Lodge, Kansas
Mrs. Flora Russell Nelson, Kansas City, Mo.
Mrs. Maxine McGuire, Attica, Kansas
Jane Ann Hargett, Anthony, Kansas
Mrs. Rufus Fraee, Anthony, Kansas
Katheryn L. Bottoreff, Harper, Kansas
Dr. and Mrs. P. J. Antrim, Anthony, Kansas
Mrs. A. A. Hilliard, Attica, Kansas
Nyle H. Miller, Secretary, Kansas State Historical Society

Mr. and Mrs. Jimmy Little, Wellington, Kansas
Dr. and Mrs. R. W. VanDeventer, Wellington, Kansas
Mr. and Mrs. Harry Jenista, Caldwell, Kansas
Mr. Chauncy McReynolds, Sharon, Kansas
Mr. and Mrs. W. G. Muir, Harper, Kansas
Betty Novall, Harper, Kansas
Orie W. Cleous, Danville, Kansas
Lawrence Maddox, Hazelton, Kansas
Chas. H. Stewart, Kingman, Kansas
Mrs. Ornie Neal, Argonia, Kansas
Mr. Ray Hayter, Anthony, Kansas
Mr. Fred T. Logan, Denver, Colorado
Mr. T. D. Hunt, Attica, Kansas
Mr. and Mrs. Ira Blasdel, Attica, Kansas
Mr. and Mrs. P. C. Miller, Belle Plaine, Kansas
Mr. and Mrs. Jess Charles, Attica, Kansas
Mr. John Crow, Anthony, Kansas
Mr. Ira Crow, Anthony, Kansas
Katheryn Kiefer, Harper, Kansas
Miss Ruby Holmes, Bluff City, Kansas
Mrs. Eva Doll, Bluff City, Kansas
Mr. and Mrs. Dale Gates, Anthony, Kansas
Mr. and Mrs. Homer Thompson, Anthony, Kansas
Mrs. Laura Whitney, Anthony, Kansas
Mr. and Mrs. F. J. Malhan, Anthony, Kansas
Mrs. Neaty Pearl, Harper, Kansas
I. L. Pfalser, Caney, Kansas
Winnona W. Pfander, Peoria, Illinois
Dorothy Scarlett, Harper, Kansas
Mr. and Mrs. Lem Laird, Harper, Kansas
Mr. and Mrs. C. C. Zollars, Harper, Kansas
Mr. and Mrs. H. F. Stalder, Harper, Kansas
R. G. Hile, New York City, N. Y., designer of medallion
J. P. Hamilton, Belle Plaine, Kansas
Mrs. Clyde Oliver, Wichita, Kansas
Mr. E. L. Atherton, Wichita, Kansas
Mr. Harris Squire, Tulsa, Oklahoma
Mr. James V. Chism, Winnipeg, Manitoba, Canada

BIBLIOGRAPHY

United States Department of Interior

Kansas State Historical Society

Harper Historical Society

The *Wichita Eagle*

The *Anthony Republican*

The *Harper Advocate*

Old newspapers of Harper County

The Kansas Turnpike Authority

Harper County Commission records

A.S.C. office, Anthony

Various city Chamber of Commerce brochures

The Attica *Independent*

Books:

Tenting on the Plains, by Elizabeth Custer
The Cherokee Strip, by George T. Rainey
Personal Recollections of General Nelson A. Miles, by General
    Nelson A. Miles
Harper County Atlases, 1886, 1902 and 1919
Kansas Historical Collection, Vol. 8
Kansas Historical Collection, Vol. 10, 1907-08
Churches in Harper County, published 1961
Diary of Theo. B. Marsh, by Theo. B. Marsh
Andrea's History, 1883
Kansas Cyclopedia, 1912